Rape of Ethiopia 1936

Rape of Ethiopia 1936

A J Barker

Editor-in-Chief: Barrie Pitt
Editor: David Mason
Art Director: Sarah Kingham
Picture Editor: Robert Hunt
Designer: David Allen
Cover: Denis Piper
Special Drawings: John Batchelor
Photographic Research: Jonathan Moore
Cartographer: Richard Natkiel

First Printing: **December** 1971
Printed in United States of America

Ballantine Books Inc.
101 Fifth Avenue New York NY 10003

An Intext Publisher

Contents

The First Brutality

Introduction by Barrie Pitt

The consequences of Mussolini's campaign in Ethiopia were more far-reaching than the mere annexing of one country to another. They were to affect the lives of millions of people – many of whom had probably never even heard of this north-east African country governed by its emperor, Haile Selassie – for undoubtedly this attempt at colonial expansion by the Italians was one of the contributory causes of the Second World War. Born out of Mussolini's dream of a new Roman Empire and of his desire to avenge a former Italian defeat at the hands of the Ethiopians at Adowa in 1896, the campaign constituted aggression of the most blatant kind with only the flimsiest of excuses given for the mobilisation of an Italian army and the subsequent crossing of the Ethiopian border.

The League of Nations, to whom Haile Selassie appealed for help, would take no direct military action to aid Ethiopia's struggle for freedom. Member states, guided by self-interest, would agree only to the imposition of minor economic sanctions against Italy, failing to restrict exports of the two commodities which might have had some effect on her conduct; an embargo on oil and coal may well have made it impossible for Mussolini to pursue his policy of Italian self-aggrandisement by force of arms.

It was ironic that such sanctions as were imposed by the League, though not comprehensive enough actually to affect Italian military efficiency, did serve to breed a certain resentment and to alienate her from Britain and France. Thus it was that, standing alone and friendless, Mussolini was receptive to the overtures of the German dictator and formed with him the Axis alliance.

As if further to flout the half-hearted opposition of the League to his vision of empire, Mussolini encouraged his military leaders to fight a campaign of great brutality in Ethiopia using all the weapons of modern warfare, including poison gas, against tribesmen armed for the most part only with rifles. Aircraft attacked towns and villages indiscriminately, dropping bombs and spraying with machine gun bullets soldier and civilian alike.

The failure of the League of Nations to grasp the nettle and take direct action against the aggression of the Italian dictator undoubtedly weakened that body as a force in world affairs; it could no longer act as a deterrent to those who would expand their influence and territorial boundaries by military means once it had been challenged and found wanting.

There were other men in Europe with dreams of empire, others who had bitter memories of past defeats to avenge, and the reluctance of the major powers within the League to do anything more than condemn the action of a nation which contemptuously ignored the very principles on which the League was founded, encouraged such men to follow a similar course. Before the resistance of the Ethiopian army had finally ceased, Adolf Hitler had occupied the demilitarized zone of the Rhineland – established by the Treaty of Versailles – and the countries of Europe found it easier to accept Hitler's word that his territorial ambitions were now sated, than to make the uncomfortable decision to take more direct action.

In Spain, General Franco fought to establish another Fascist dictatorship, and appealed to the Duce for help. Italians were sent as volunteers to support the Fascist cause and were followed by men sent by Hitler. Hitler also used the Spanish Civil War as a proving ground for the developing Luftwaffe, honing the cutting edge of the weapon he was preparing for use on a complacent Europe – air power supporting armour and assault troops, the Blitzkreig.

The success of Italian arms in Ethiopia led Mussolini to believe that he could quickly win any war that he might choose to undertake. It was this belief, and the adultation of the Italian people who gave him their support now that the Ethiopian war was satisfactorily concluded, which encouraged him to attempt the disastrous policies which led eventually, via unsuccessful conquest, to ignominious defeat and surrender without honour.

A J Barker gives a comprehensive account of the campaign and its immediate aftermath, from the insignificant incident at Wal Wal in December 1934 used by Mussolini as his excuse for invasion, until after Graziani's removal from the position of Viceroy of Ethiopia in 1937. It is a tale of bitter fighting, of savage battles in which the Ethiopians suffered three times more casualties than they were able to inflict on the Italian forces; of the ruthless use of air power, and of the widespread use of poison gas. The years of occupation following the end of the war, commenced with a term of savage oppression imposed by Graziani which quickly alienated any pro-Italian sympathies there may have been in certain sections of the populace; by the time his successor, the Duke of Aosta, took office it was too late to make amends.

The Italian nation payed dearly for its attempts to build a latter-day Roman Empire, and for its brief espousal of Fascism. It must surely be a damaging indictment of any political creed, when under its régime, a nation conducts itself in a barbarous and inhumane manner foreign to its national character.

Mussolini looks toward conquest

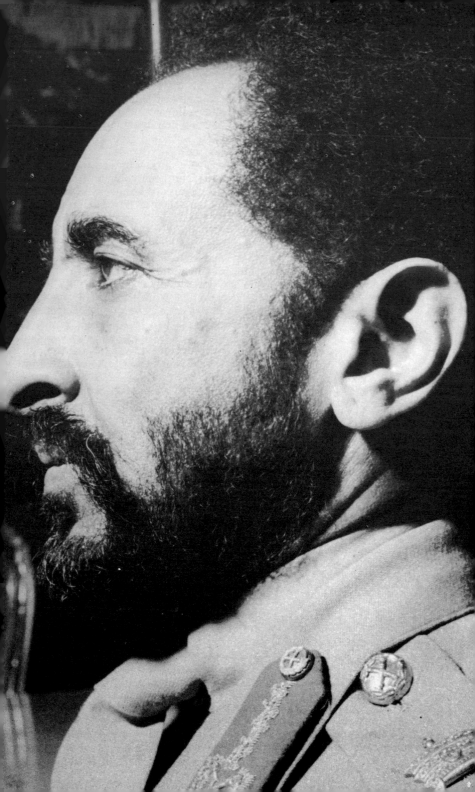

'Imperialism is the eternal and immutable law of life. All considered, it is only the need, the wish and the will to expand each individual that each lively and vital people carries in itself' – Mussolini, January 1919.

Surrounded by the monuments of ancient Roman glories, the Palazzo Venezia stands in the heart of Rome. Built in the fashion of a mediaeval castle in the 15th century, the building dominates the great piazza which lies before it. Here, in a historic and grandiose setting, Benito Mussolini, Italy's Fascist Duce, had his headquarters. And it was here that the modern Caesar dreamed of a new Roman Empire. In the beginning, this

A feudal chief . . .

empire would be colonial, and come by way of conquest, for only as such would it be justified in the eyes of the world. This, the Duce reasoned, was the pattern that all mighty nations had followed in the past. Thus his actions would be morally justified,and their outcome would redress the injustice perpetrated at Versailles, where – though on the winning side – Italy had been robbed of her share of the spoils. It would cure the Italians of the sense of frustration they continued to feel, and it would also provide a much-needed outlet for Italy's growing population. Finally, it would bring glory and the awed recognition of the world.

In Mussolini's reasoning logic and muddled thinking were always mixed. It was true that in the past civilised nations had conquered lands and earned wealth by subjugating backward peoples; yet after the First World War – the war to end all wars – the building of empires had been forsworn. Colonial exploitation was going out of fashion and the trend was towards the independence of existing colonies rather than the seizing of new ones. It was also the time that Italy attracted a certain amount of sympathy for the ill-treatment she had received at Versailles, and it was generally recognised that the Italian colonies, Libya, Eritrea and Italian Somaliland, were no asset, being little more than a collection of deserts. All the same, this did not mean that more successful empire builders would consider Italy morally entitled to acquire new colonies in Africa by force of arms. When the United States, Canada and Australia passed stricter immigration laws after the First World War, Italy's emigration problem was undoubtedly exacerbated. And Mussolini could well argue that a colonial empire would absorb his surplus population without the loss of Italian nationals to foreign countries. Yet the need for an empire could hardly be a reason for the encouragement of an increase in population to which the country was committed in order to multiply the 'eight million bayonets' of which he boasted.

Having decided that an empire was Italy's goal, it was inevitable that Mussolini's eyes should turn to Africa and focus on Ethiopia, the only African country that had preserved independence from white rule. It was a vast country, almost impenetrable for lack of roads and railways, with no access to the sea except by way of the only railroad from Addis Ababa, the capital, to the port of Djibouti in French Somaliland; a country in which enormous stretches of torrid desert and barren, stony plateaux alternated with green and luxuriant lands; where there were lions, leopards, hyenas, lynx and wolves; of whose vast mineral deposits much was said and very little was known definitely; a country whose main exports were coffee and hides. Yet Ethiopia was the logical object of Mussolini's imperialistic ambitions. It bordered on the Italian colonies of Eritrea to the north and Somaliland to the south-east; for decades it had been recognised by the European colonial powers as in the Italian sphere of influence. Furthermore

... of a backward country which Mussolini considered needed the 'benefits' of western civilisation

July 1924. Haile Selassie (then Ras
Tafari, Regent of Ethiopia) with the
Duke of York on a formal visit to the
King at Buckingham Palace. 'Ethiopia'
he claimed, 'is like Sleeping Beauty
waking after 2,000 years of sleep'

926. His nose bandaged after an
attempt on his life, Mussolini leaves for
a visit to poverty-stricken Tripoli which
convinces him that Ethiopia is the only
proper victim available for Italian
colonisation

Count Dino Grandi, the Italian Ambassador in London. He confided Italy's secret preparations for war to the British government to see which way the wind was blowing

Sir John Simon, British Foreign Minister. He made it readily apparent that Britain would to little to help Ethiopia

there was an Italian account left over from 1896 to be settled.

When Menelik became Negus of Ethiopia in 1889, he signed a treaty of friendship with Italy, a treaty he soon denounced to attack Italian troops stationed on soil annexed from Ethiopia. In the battle of Adowa that ensued, the Italians were defeated by a native army eight times their strength; and the Ethiopians perpetrated the most barbarous atroci-

ties on Italian prisoners. When thi happened Benito Mussolini wa thirteen years old and at school; an the news of the Italian defeat was severe blow to his impressionabl mind. Fifteen years later he wrote the casualty figures of the disastrou battle – 10,000 dead and seventy-tw cannon lost – were still hammering i his skull.

As a child Mussolini nursed th national grievance; as a dictator h had the means for revenge. He signe treaties with Britain and France, pledging to preserve the status quo in Ethiopia and defining the spheres of influence of each country. With Ethiopia he signed a treaty – a two year pact of 'Friendship, Conciliation, and Arbitration'. But treaties were not brakes on his actions. He was always ready to enter into agreements with any country willing to sign pacts of friendship, or trade, or mutual security, because it enhanced Italy's importance in the world. Not that Mussolini regarded any such agreements as binding: treaties were, he said repeatedly, not 'eternal' but bound to be 'revised' – which in the Duce's mind meant they were subject to change, including complete violation, if it suited his purpose. The memory of the Adowa defeat was longer lasting and more impelling than any treaty provision. 'The great account opened in 1896', Mussolini declared in 1935, 'had to be settled at all costs.' Then his Roman dream would become reality.

Other considerations may have come to Mussolini's mind: his determination to leave a deeper imprint in history than any great Italian before him; his belief that an empire might truly prove economically advantageous, especially since the world depression had begun to threaten Italy's precarious economy, and – together with the forced, artificial value of the lira – had caused foreign trade to decline; and the fact that he had run out of propaganda stunts to occupy the Italian people and keep the Fascists happily busy. His last great performance on the Fascist stage had been the reconciliation of the party with the Vatican. In the rôle of empire builder before the world, he could also include the part of bearer of the true faith to the tribes of Ethiopia belonging to the Coptic Church. This, the Duce correctly surmised, would please the Vatican and obtain, if not its blessing, its support. Thus in the early 'thirties Mussolini talked of peace and pre-pared for war.

Within the space of three years the colonial enterprise became Mussolini's sole concern. He usually saw only one side of any question, and he let the colonial campaign overshadow the troubles of Europe, the rise of Adolf Hitler and the Nazi threat to the world, the advantages that Italy might have obtained from Britain and France, and the Italian pledge to abide by the rulings of the League of Nations. Apparently he had forgotten the dire consequences of the Libyan War of 1911 which he himself had opposed. Nor did he remember the unpreparedness of the army and the nation when Italy entered the First World War. In his one-sided stubbornness he does not seem to have worried about the enormous cost of a long and questionable colonial campaign thousands of miles away, and it seems that he did not realise – or did not stop to consider – that a colony is a long-term investment whose dividends are slow to mature. The Duce had made up his mind and he was not going to change it.

It would be difficult to pinpoint the date when the Duce first considered the conquest of Ethiopia. From all the available evidence most historians agree that it was some time in 1932. Yet there is some reason to believe that he had been toying with the idea as far back as 1925. The alternative of a colonising expansion in the sandbox of Italian Somaliland was never a serious consideration, and a visit to Tripoli in 1926 quickly convinced Mussolini that the other wretchedly poor colony which might have provided opportunities for expansion could also be ruled out. From this time on, Ethiopia was the only victim in the Italian sights, and Mussolini began to discreetly sound out the diplomatic climate in Europe, while he prepared to strike. Meanwhile Italian agents in East Africa embarked on a clandestine campaign in Ethiopia, to corrupt and win over some of the dissident rulers and tribes of Emperor Haile Selassie's loosely-knit empire. These men did their work well and when the war came, a good third of the Ethiopian army was paralysed. Rases and notables who bore some grudge against the Emperor bent over backwards in their anxiety to cause the Italians no trouble.

Early in 1932 Mussolini summoned the aging General Emilio de Bono, one of his loyal and devoted followers, to the Palazzo Venezia. The Duce asked de Bono to go to Eritrea and 'see how matters stand'. Although the mission went unnoticed in Europe its purpose was soon to become obvious. The 'irrevocable decision' had been taken and Mussolini was making plans for the invasion which he later sought to convince the world was unpremeditated.

In September King Victor Emmanuel followed up with a state visit to the 'first-born colony', toured its battlefields and pronounced himself 'deeply moved' by the homage of the disabled Eritrean soldiers who had fought under the Italian flag at Adowa. In 1932 also the Italian High Command revised project OME – the defensive-offensive plan for Eritrea in the event of war. Mussolini had told several of the Fascist hierarchy of his 'Grand Design' by this time and the news was spreading. Count Dino Grandi, the Italian ambassador at the Court of St James, even confided the secret to Sir John Simon – possibly in order to find out which way the wind was

blowing in Britain. A year later, sixty-eight year old de Bono was told that he could regard himself as Commander-in-Chief of the forthcoming 'operations'. There were still two years to go but Mussolini already had a plan of campaign and a Commander-in-Chief to carry it out.

The decision which may be regarded as the point of no return was taken in December 1934, when an incident at Wal Wal provided Mussolini with a pretext to mobilise.

Wal Wal is a watering place in the desert near what was then the Italian Somaliland border with Ethiopia. According to all the maps in current use it was well inside Ethiopia, but the border between the Italian colony and Haile Selassie's territory had never been properly delineated. For reasons which were never clearly determined there was a skirmish between the Italian garrison of Somalis who were in the Duce's service, and a force of armed Ethiopians. According to the Italians ten days later, the Ethiopians attacked the Somalis with machine guns; according to the Ethiopian version the Italians, supported by two tanks and three aircraft, attacked them. The sound of firing round the wells had scarcely died away when Mussolini was demanding apologies and reparations. Barely a week later the Duce sent de Bono to Ethiopia as High Commissioner – a title he exchanged in March for one more significant and provocative: Commander-in-Chief of the Italian army in Africa.

If only because border incidents were common enough in colonial territories it was patently clear that Mussolini had seized on what had happened at Wal Wal to prepare openly for war. British and French colonial authorities usually handled similar affairs with a subaltern and a few native troops; and the world outside rarely heard about them. But the Duce had made up his mind that Wal Wal should be the *casus belli* and so the Italian press was ordered to give it front-page headlines – featuring the incident as a deliberate and provocative aggression on the part of Ethiopia, an act so grave that it could not be condoned. A month later, the Arbitration Committee appointed by the League of Nations was compelled to admit that after extreme extensive inquiries it could not apportion blame for the incident. Not only, then, did the question of who had provoked the fighting remain unanswerable, but it was also doubtful whether Italy had a

De Bono leads the Italian High Command rapidly towards mobilisation after Mussolini seizes on a minor border incident at Wal Wal in December 1934 as a pretext to prepare openly for war

17

Ethiopia's feudal chiefs rally in support of their Emperor, but Haile Selassie, with his pathetic faith in the League of Nations, delayed mobilisation until September 1935

legitimate right to be in Wal Wal at all.

Mussolini was not concerned about technical or juridical niceties, however; his mind was wholly engaged by the prospect of the imminent conquest of Ethiopia. Not only would it provide Italy with a new outlet for her shrinking export trade and a partial solution of her critical unemployment problem by the redeployment on the vast Amharan uplands of a large proportion of the redundant labour force, but it would also furnish the Duce with what he wanted – war. This he needed to prove the Roman virility of his people and to show the world that his Fascist regime brought material success. In a speech at Bologna a few months earlier he had boasted that Italy was '. . . becoming a mili-

tary nation . . . and to complete it *warlike . . .*'

Emperor Haile Selassie protested to the League of Nations. In doing so he took a step that broke all tradition in the pattern of relations between European and African peoples. But this did not deter Mussolini. On 5th and 11th February 1935 the mobilisation of two army divisions, the *Gavinana* and the *Peloritana*, was ordered, and when the Duce received a letter dated 13th February from de Bono informing him that '. . . at present the Negusa Negast is ordering too many prayers and fasts to give us reason to think he wishes to attack us . . .' he showed his contempt for the League of Nations by replying, 'If the Negus does not intend to attack us, we ourselves must take the initiative'. In a subsequent letter to his Commander-in-Chief he wrote, 'You ask for three divisions by the end of October; I mean to send you ten, repeat ten: five divisions of the regular army, five formations of Black-

The prospect of a colonial adventure
was immensely popular in Italy,
especially with the numerous
unemployed to whom it meant a job
and a patch of land

The *SS Cesare Batista* at Port Said with reinforcements for the Italian troops massing on the Ethiopian border

shirts. For the lack of a few thousand men, we lost the day at Adowa. We shall never make that mistake. I am willing to commit a sin of excess, but never a sin of deficiency.'

Mussolini was as good as his word. On 8th April the first battalion of the *Gavinana* disembarked at Massawa, and during the next few months five army and five Blackshirt divisions arrived in East Africa via the Suez canal. One division and a few Blackshirt battalions were assigned to General Graziani, Commander of the Forces in Italian Somaliland, but the main build-up was in Eritrea. This first expeditionary force comprised more than 200,000 men and 7,000 officers, 6,000 machine guns, 700 pieces of artillery, 150 tanks, and 150 aircraft. The flood of troops into Africa reached its height in September when General Baistrocchi, Under Secretary for War, informed the Senate that from Naples alone 100,000 men, 1,000,000 tons of stores and ammunition, 200 cannon, 6,000 mules and 2,300 motor vehicles had been shipped overseas. Faced with this staggering influx of men and materials, General de Bono was compelled to ask the Duce for a 10,000 strong labour force (the figure was soon to rise to 50,000), to improve the port of Massawa, resurface the road from Massawa to the Eritrean capital, Asmara, and build other roads and accommodation for the huge army that was now assembling. The General's request gratified various federal secretaries who rid their provinces once and for all of the chronic unemployed, but when the first squads arrived de Bono was anything but pleased. 'Just anyone was sent out', he said. But his Quartermaster-General Dall'Ora dealt brilliantly with the complex problems of provisioning, billeting and transport and on 2nd October 1935 the stage was set for the invasion. From his headquarters in the centre

of Asmara, whose every street was jammed with troops and their impedimenta, de Bono issued his final instructions. Five days earlier he had received a peremptory telegram from the Duce: 'Order you to attack at dawn on third, repeat third October.' De Bono had planned to strike on 5th October but loyal servant that he was, he obeyed without demur.

Both in Eritrea and Italian Somaliland, all preparations were now complete and Mussolini might well have congratulated himself on the speed and efficiency with which the expeditionary force had been organised. But the Duce was too preoccupied by the turn events had taken in Europe. For several months he had been fairly convinced that the treaty signed by

Laval in Rome on 7th January 1935 had cleared all the obstacles which lay in the path of his enterprise. But he had failed to take account of Britain. At first it appeared that the British government, which was preparing for an election, was prepared to let matters go their own way. Anthony Eden (Lord Avon) as Minister for League Affairs, was then the British symbol of interest in the new principles of internationalism and collective security through the League. At the end of June Eden visited Mussolini and proposed a peaceful settlement to the Ethiopian question. The Duce found Eden's proposal to be unacceptable, however, and shortly after Eden's unfortunate trip to Rome the results of a 'peace ballot' were published in Britain. This indicated that public opinion in Britain was in favour of applying sanctions against aggressors. This put matters in a different light, and Britain's Conservative government adopted a more resolute policy towards Italy. The new attitude reached its culminating point on 20th September when the British Mediterranean Fleet was reinforced.

But the threat implied by this move did not deter Mussolini from pressing on with his preparations for a land campaign in Ethiopia (especially when the Italian Intelligence Service [SIM] reported that the British Mediterranean Fleet was not properly equipped). To a vast crowd packed into Piazza Venezia on 8th September, he thundered, 'And now, at the end of this stirring day, I come to the words you have been waiting to hear: we shall go straight ahead.' And to a British journalist ten days later he ranted, 'We have an army in East Africa which has cost us two billion lire. Do you really believe that we have spent such an astronomical sum for nothing? We are on the march . . .' Meanwhile the Italian newspapers vied with one another to depict the Ethiopians as savages who had forfeited their right to exist as a nation.

In the eyes of the world the forthcoming campaign was anything but popular. But in Italy it was a diff-

September 1935. Italian war planes packed for transport on the quay at Naples

ferent story. The appearance of the British fleet in the Mediterranean and the economic sanctions imposed by the League of Nations only increased the people's enthusiasm for the war. As R Zangrandi, an Italian writer whose work is not tainted with Fascist sympathy, wrote in *Il lungo viaggio attraverso il fascismo*, 'The vast majority of Italians, particularly the younger generation, hailed the colonial enterprise with sincere enthusiasm. They were fighting for a place in the sun that other great powers had enjoyed for years or for centuries, and to a country as poor and overpopulated as Italy, the conquest of Ethiopia meant jobs and a patch of land for millions of unfortunates.'

Thirteen years of Fascist propaganda and indoctrination had made an

indelible mark on all Italians, especially on the younger generation. When Mussolini made his solemn declaration, sirens sounded, church bells pealed throughout Italy and the population was seized with a fit of nationalistic frenzy. Shouting and cheering, many of them rushed into the streets and squares in a passionate patriotic stampede comparable only with the demonstrations before Caesar in the days of the old Roman Empire. The young conscript soldiers who sailed from Italy in 1935 sincerely believed they were off to champion the rights of their own downtrodden nation, or that they were going on a civilising mission to a country oppressed by a feudal regime. Peasants from southern Italy flocked to Ethiopia because they could earn 45

The conscript soldiers who sailed from Italy in 1935 earnestly believed that they were going on a civilising mission to a country oppressed by a feudal régime

lire a day – as much as they could earn in a week at home. Members of the Fascist hierarchy rushed off to Africa to win fame and fortune; industrialists supported the campaign because of the profits it promised. Apart from the anti-Fascists who lived in exile abroad not a single Italian raised his voice to denounce Mussolini's venture. Even the attitude of the Vatican was ambiguous. Pope Pius declared on 28th August 1935 that 'the very thought of this war is abhorrent to me . . .' But quite a number of his senior prelates gave the war their blessing.

23

Ethiopian viewpoint

When John Melly, the medical missionary who was to die in Haile Selassie's service, arrived in Addis Ababa in 1934 he was aghast at what he saw. The capital of Ethiopia was a huddle of mud *tukuls* daubed with whitewash and a few brick-built oriental style houses. Only one passable hotel, the Imperial, existed and the only tarmac road was the one which had been surfaced for the Negus's coronation. There were no drains, and refuse was simply dumped into the streets, to be cleared by the vultures and crows or more simply to rot. By and large such conditions were to be found in other parts of Africa, of course, including regions

frontiers of Ethiopia first began to show signs of their intentions, the Negus had only just embarked on his programme of centralisation and modernisation. In November 1930 he drew up the country's first penal code; a year later, he produced its first written constitution and outlined his plans for significant administrative reforms. To carry these out, he enlisted the help of foreign experts – Everett Colson of America, General Virgin of Sweden, de Halpert of Great Britain, and Auberson of Switzerland. Outwardly, the changes were so slow as to be almost imperceptible, but this was because Haile Selassie was opposed to any sudden and radical reforms. Ethiopia, he maintained, was like 'Sleeping Beauty' waking after 2,000 years of sleep.

Haile Selassie did not wish to overwhelm his people. He also had to contend with the reactionay influence of the Coptic clergy who were averse to any kind of change, and the pressure exerted by his rases who regarded any attempt at reform as a direct threat to themselves. As it was impossible for him to rid himself of these two power groups, the traditional pillars of his throne, he was compelled to move with the utmost caution. Thus Italian propagandists were able to make great play of his apparent dilatoriness and according to them the Emperor was just a puppet in the hands of greedy nobles. But it was primarily on the question of slavery that Haile Selassie was pilloried. At the beginning of the 'thirties this scourge was still widespread in Ethiopia and there were reckoned to be upwards of half a million people held in bondage.

Trying to extirpate an evil that was deeply rooted in the customs of the

hich had been colonised by white settlers. But an objective observer would have been compelled to admit that the task of modernizing Ethiopia which Haile Selassie had set himself seemed almost hopeless – taking into consideration the vastness of the country, the lack of roads and communications and above all the power wielded by the reactionary and ambitious rases.

Given time there is little doubt that the energetic little Emperor with the iron will who had been born Ras Tafari would have transformed his country and brought it into the 20th century without the help of the Italians. But when the Italians on the

As soldiers guard the Royal Palace in Addis Ababa, Italian propagandists pillory Haile Selassie for the 500,000 slaves said to exist in his country

country was no easy task. Nevertheless while he was still regent, the Negus had taken steps to abolish slavery. In September 1923 he had issued a decree making the buying and selling of slaves a crime punishable by death. Six months later he had announced in an edict that the children of slaves would be born free and that on the death of their master all slaves would be given their liberty. Finally, in 1934 the Emperor had set up a bureau in Addis Ababa for the repression of slavery, and two years later sixty-two similar centres had been opened in the country. Unfortunately, the results had been negligible and the Italian government could flatter itself it had scored a point when the League of Nations – after an open controversy with the Negus – decided, on 22nd May

35, to publish the latest secret report [o]f the Advisory Committee on Slavery. [T]his report came down with particular [s]everity on Ethiopia. But it was [tr]ansparently clear that Italy's satis[fa]ction at these revelations was [in]spired by the fact that they played [in]to her hands and not by genuine [m]oral indignation.

From 1929 onward, duly warned that [It]aly was showing her intentions more [an]d more plainly, Haile Selassie had [ta]ken certain precautions. Ethiopians [se]rving in Britain's King's African [R]ifles had been recalled from Kenya, [th]e Imperial Guard were being drilled [an]d instructed by officers of the [Be]lgian Military Mission and the [E]mperor had asked General Virgin to [se]t up a military academy for the [tr]aining of cadets who would form a [ca]dre of officers for the army. But on [th]e eve of the war, the army had not [m]ade much progress, a fact that was [du]ly noted by the Italian Supreme [C]ommand in East Africa. In a manual [C]ommando Superiore A O Stato Maggiore, Ufficio Informazioni, 'Riservato'. *Etiopia: Guida practica per l'ufficiale destinato in Africa Orientale*) marked 'confidential' it was noted that, 'all but the human element can be discounted. The Ethiopian soldier needs little, is tough and zealous of his honour. He is such a fanatical fighter that in the heat of battle he is utterly oblivious of death.' In the event this desperate courage proved to be pitifully inadequate against the weight of ten divisions, equipped with modern arms and commanded by modern tactical experts, supported by an excellent air force and artillery as well as by flamethrowers, and – as if this was not enough – by gas.

'We did not even contemplate fighting a European-style war , Haile Selassie said subsequently. 'Moreover,

Drum-major Belu Abaka, over seven feet tall, parades with the Imperial band as part of the war demonstrations which were temporarily interrupted when the Emperor's lions escaped

Ethiopia and Italy's possessions before the war

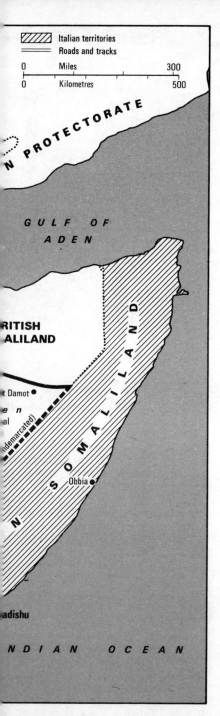

it would have been impossible as what we had in the way of artillery, even machine guns, was laughable.' The Italians estimated – overestimated, according to the Ethiopians – that on the eve of hostilities the enemy had an army of 350,000 men (of whom only a quarter had had any kind of military training); 400,000 rifles of every type and in every kind of condition; 200 antiquated pieces of artillery mounted on rigid gun carriages; about 50 light and heavy anti-aircraft guns, Oerlikons, .75 Schneiders and Vickers; and a mixed batch of Ford and Fiat-3000 armoured cars. The regulars of the Imperial Guard were fitted out in the greenish khaki uniforms of the Belgian army, but their berets had been made in Japan; the rest of the troops wore the white *shamma* (the Ethiopian cotton cloak), and an excellent target it proved to be.

Modest and ill-equipped as this army was, the Negus waited until 28th September before giving the order to mobilize. He could not bring himself to give up hope that the dispute would be settled peacefully and he had a pathetic faith in the League of Nations as well as in the sympathy extended to him by the pro-Ethiopian committees that had been set up in countries all over the world as a protest against Italy's belligerent attitude. Most of the European countries other than Italy had active protest groups; that in London was organised by Sylvia Pankhurst who devoted herself tirelessly to the Emperor's cause. But the most vehement outbursts of indignation provoked by Italy's threatening attitude towards Ethiopia came from the cities where there was an elite of educated Africans from the United States, the Caribbean and the capitals of the British dominions in Africa. To the coloured people of the world Ethiopia was the last free bastion of African culture – a kind of black Zion – whose independence had

The Palazzo Venezia, 2nd October 1935.
Blackshirted fascists wait for
Mussolini to make the famous speech
from the balcony declaring war

to be maintained at all costs. In fact
a number of semi-religious cults,
whose adherents revered Haile
Selassie and regarded Ethiopia as the
'promised land', came into being in the
'twenties. These cults were known as
'ethiopianism' or took the regent's
name and title – hence the Rasta-
farians.

But all the vociferous support of
Ethiopia's 'friends' could not stop the
Fascist war machine, and Haile
Selassie reluctantly came to recognize
that an Italian invasion was inevit-
able. His task now was to prepare the
country for the struggle that lay
ahead. On 18th July he broadcast from
Ethiopia's only radio station at
Akaki, telling his people that he

would never agree to the proposa
that Ethiopia should become a
Italian protectorate. On 12th Augus
the Negus addressed his subjects again
'Italy', he said, 'continues to pou
men and arms into Eritrea and Italia
Somaliland. The danger of an arme
conflict increases hour by hour.'

On 15th September, after Italy ha
turned down the proposals for
peaceful settlement put forward b
the League of Nations' Committee o
Five, the Emperor was at the micro
phone again: 'Today, when it ha
been made absolutely clear that th
Wal Wal incident provides no ground
for war, Italy, who has been supplie
with arms and munitions by power
that have denied them to our countr
– which has never manufactured wa
materials and desperately needs then
for self-defence – Italy is seeking t
discredit our government and ou
people in the eyes of the world b

asserting that we are savages whom it is her duty to civilize. The attitude that Italy has seen fit to assume will be judged by history.' Two days earlier the Empress Menen had made a radio appeal to the women of every country, calling for their support: 'The wives and mothers of Italy are as anguished as the wives and mothers of Ethiopia at the thought of all the agony and suffering war would bring upon them. Women of the world, unite! Demand with one voice that we may be spared the horror of useless bloodshed.'

In Italy, regimental colours were being blessed with 'holy water from the Piave', and a 'Fascist Sabbath' had been introduced to work up patriotic fervour. The Emperor's broadcasts had a similar effect on Ethiopians, and an orgy of patriotic speeches and displays developed. In Harar *Waizero* (Lady) Ababath Charkoze, the daughter of a wealthy landowner, organized a 'Battalion of Death', and was photographed in uniform clutching a rifle to her stomach. Another *waizero* told the correspondent of Britain's *Daily Express* in Addis that she had recuited a 'Legion of Amazons', and had already enrolled 3,000 recruits. A redoutable old woman, Ferlenek, who forty years earlier had fought against the Italians at Adowa, posed in front of the press cameras aiming a pistol at an invisible enemy. Only on 25th September was the war fever temporarily forgotten: the Emperor's lions had escaped from their cages and the panic-stricken people rushed to take cover. But as soon as they learned that the last of the animals had been shot by the Imperial Guard, they returned to their demonstrations, as the drum-major, Belu Abaka – a giant of a man, and over six feet tall – paraded with the imperial band twirling his baton with consummate skill. On 27th September came the feast of Maskal, a religious feast which marks the end of the rainy season in Ethiopia. After the religious ceremony in St George's Cathedral the Emperor seated himself in a magnificent pavilion specially erected for the occasion in the cathedral square. Headed by a veteran of Adowa, whose antics were intended to recall the heroic deeds of Ethiopia's past, a military procession filed past the Negus. Overhead flew the three tiny and outmoded biplanes which constituted the serviceable element of the Emperor's air force.

War was only five days away; and in these last remaining days of peace the statesmen of the five continents thought and spoke of little else but the imminent clash. Intuitively they realized that the Italo-Ethiopian conflict would be the prologue to a second world war. In Britain 3,000 young men volunteered to fight for Haile Selassie, in New York, 9,000 Americans – white and black alike – staged a rally in Madison Square Garden and tore a huge effigy of Mussolini to shreds. In Berlin cinemas were showing 'Ethiopia 1935', a film through which ran an anti-Italian theme, while in London long queues formed in Coventry Street to see 'The Truth about Abyssinia' at the Rialto. In Cairo the muezzin called the faithful to pray to Allah that Ethiopia might be spared. Astrologers and seers unanimously predicted Italy would win the war, and one of them declared that no power on earth could prevent the war from breaking out because it was foretold in the Bible in Isaiah, Habakkuk and Zechariah.

And, in fact, at 6.45pm, on 2nd October, the last, lingering hopes crumbled to dust. From the balcony of the Palazzo Venezia, Mussolini addressed the vast crowd that had been summoned to the square by the wailing of sirens and the pealing of bells: 'At this moment, forty million Italians have gathered in the piazzas of every city, town and village. Never in the history of mankind has such a tremendous spectacle been seen.' It was the end. After the rape of Ethiopia, it would be the rape of Spain, the rape of Poland. Thereafter, all Europe from the Urals to the Pyrenees would be ablaze.

De Bono's
war

At noon on 2nd October 1935, Mussolini strode out on to the balcony of the Palazzo Venezia and told the world that Italy's patience with Ethiopia was finally exhausted. Seven hours before this fateful announcement General Emilio de Bono had left the sumptuous governor-general's palace in Asmara and driven to the tiny Eritrean village of Coatit. There, within a few miles of the muddy slow-moving Mareb river delineating the Ethiopian border, a cluster of tents had been set up to serve the Army Commander as tactical headquarters. Three army corps waited for the order to cross the Mareb and advance into Ethiopia. De Bono was to issue this order in the early hours of 3rd October. But even before de Bono reached Coatit, Emperor Haile Selassie in Addis Ababa was cabling the Secretary-General of the League of Nations to complain that Italian troops had already violated the Ethiopian frontier, and ordering Ras Seyoum, commander of the Ethiopian Tigre Army, to withdraw 'a day's march from the River Mareb before the Italians cross it.' The Negus was determined to show the world who was the aggressor.

Although the Mareb has the status of a river, the trickle of water which flows between bare foothills can hardly be classified as an obstacle. But to the 100,000 men who reached it shortly after de Bono's order had been issued, it had a shameful significance. This was the border that had been imposed by Menelik after the shattering defeat of the Italians at Adowa. Thus, to the young Italian conscripts – the oldest were of the 1911 class – crossing the Mareb was symbolic. They were avenging the dead of Adowa, hurling defiance at the colonial powers whose governments opposed the war, and showing the world that a new generation of Italians were just as good soldiers as the old Roman legionnaires.

At precisely 5am de Bono's three columns crossed the Mareb on a forty-mile front. On the right, the II Army Corps under General Maravigna began its advance on Adowa. In the centre General Pirzio Biroli's Eritrean Corps moved off toward the mountains of Enticho. On the left, the I Army Corps commanded by General Santini had Adigrat as its objective. Each man had been issued with 110 rounds of ammunition, four days' rations, and two litres of water. As the sun came up the three columns advanced into Ethiopia with banners flying and trumpets blaring triumphantly. Carried away by the delirious excitement of the Italians, some of the Eritrean Askaris discharged their rifles into the air. Not another shot disturbed the utter tranquility of the first day of the war.

At this stage of the campaign there was only one drawback once the Mareb had been crossed. The Italians had built roads up to the frontier on their side of the river. But in the Ethiopian territory only vaguely-defined paths existed and wheels were useless; from here on the Duce's troops had to march.

On the second day these columns were still marching, and there had been no resistance. Haile Selassie had decided to demonstrate his adherence to the conditions imposed on him by the League of Nations. He had also decided to follow the customary Ethiopian tactics of luring the enemy deep into Ethiopian territory and so further away from his supply lines, before he struck. Ras Gugsa and Ras Seyoum, commanding the Ethiopian forces in the area, were ordered to establish a defence line thirty-five and fifty-five miles from the frontier. As this meant abandoning Adowa some of the tradition-minded Ethiopians resented the order to pull back. But Haile Selassie was intent on respecting the twenty-mile neutral zone fixed by the League of Nations.

In actual fact Ras Seyoum had disobeyed the Emperor and had sent two small forces into the 'neutral zone' where one established itself at Daro Takle and the other at the

The Imperial Guard, best equipped of all Ethiopian formations, in training. They were helped by a Belgian military mission

Gashorki Pass. But they held out for only a few hours and, on the evening of 4th October, Ras Seyoum Mangasha abandoned his modest *gebbi* on the summit of the hill that dominates Adowa, and took refuge in a cave at Maryam Shoaitu. From this hideout on the following day he witnessed a wanton and bloody bombing of Adowa. From now on the roads were wide open for the invasion. Ras Seyoum withdrew, while Ras Gugsa had turned traitor and was seeking to make contact with the enemy. On 5th October Adigrat capitulated – without a single shot being fired. Next day it was Adowa, which, like Adigrat, offered no resistance.

With the fall of these two cities Adowa was 'avenged'. The Italian soldiers were wild with joy, but when the feverish excitement induced by the fanfares of trumpets and ringing patriotic speeches had subsided, they began to realize that Adowa and Adigrat were just two miserable little villages and some of them, with that commonsense that characterizes the working class, began to ask themselves whether it was really worthwhile fighting a war to occupy them. In any case they felt it was pointless to behave like conquerors to these poor Tigreans who overflowed with gratitude if they were given an empty wine bottle. Fraternization was the order of the day and General de Bono himself lost no time in establishing peaceful relations with the population. On 14th October he issued a proclamation ordering the suppression of slavery. When very little came of it de Bono began to appreciate the difficulties that had beset the Emperor in his efforts to rid Ethiopia of this evil. 'If the absolute truth be told,' he wrote, 'I am obliged to say that the proclamation did not have much effect on the owners of slaves and perhaps still less on the liberated slaves themselves. Many of the latter, the instant they were set free presented themselves to the Italian authorities, asking "And now who gives me food?"' '

During the afternoon of 11th October 'General' Haile Selassie Gugsa (his real title was *Dejagmateh* – Commander of the Door – a royal appointment) and 1,200 of his followers surrendered to the commander of the Italian outpost at Adagamos. De Bono notified Rome, where the Ministry of Information promptly exaggerated the importance of Gugsa's defection for public consumption. Because he was the son-in-law of the Negus the event was important but as he had persuaded less than a tenth of his army to defect with him the event was not critical. Two weeks before the invasion the Negus had been warned that Gugsa was not to be trusted, and was shown evidence suggesting he was already in the pay of the Italians. But Emperor Haile Selassie had shrugged, observed that 'most of the rases take money from the Italians', and refused to remove Gugsa from his command.

Despite the Negus's view that his people were prone to bribery without corruption, the financial preparations so carefully laid by Italian agents in Tigre were now beginning to pay off. On 15th October the chapter of the Cathedral of Axum presented itself in Adowa to make a solemn act of submission. Two days later this was followed by the bloodless occupation of the holy city of the Copts, and de Bono rode in on a white horse, to the tumultuous applause of the population. As the Italian ex-policeman and Commander-in-Chief sensed, the purpose of this ovation was to mitigate the rigours of the occupation, and was not – as Italian propagandists asserted – clear evidence that the people of that part of the world were devoid of patriotic feeling. Indeed, at this stage of the war the desertion of large numbers of Eritrean Askaris who went over to the Ethiopians – so ultimately signing their own death warrants – suggested the contrary. The Italians had pursued a deliberate policy of fanning the traditional flame

of hatred between Somalis and Ethiopians, Eritreans and Ethiopians, Moslems and Copts. But the fact that Somalis and Eritreans fought together under the banner of the Lion of Judah in a desperate attempt to hold back the most powerful invasion force Africa had ever seen, may serve as an indication of Africa's nascent nationalism.

In the course of a few months the desertion of the Eritrean colonial troops was to assume serious proportions, indeed, on Graziani's southern front 904 Askaris deserted in a single night, but de Bono barely had time to appreciate the significance of this problem before he was relieved of his command. Mussolini, stung by the mounting condemnation of the League of Nations, had concluded that his colonial commander was moving far too slowly. The Duce needed glittering victories, and he needed them fast. In Rome he was not prepared to hear of obstacles or delays in the theatre of operations, and a mission comprising the Colonial Secretary, Alessandro Lessona, and the Chief of Staff, Marshal Badoglio, was sent to Eritrea to see what could be done to speed things up. According to Lessona, Mussolini had already decided, before the 'mission' left Italy, that de Bono had outlived his usefulness as Commander-in-Chief.

Even before Lessona and Badoglio had left Italy on their mission, the Duce was bombarding de Bono with telegrams urging action. After the

November the first patrols entered the town. In Italy this fresh success brought great acclamations: the Duce had been right, it seemed – as always. But from the military point of view the advance had been a grave mistake because it left the flank of the Italian army completely uncovered.

Yet Mussonini's appetite for victories was still not satisfied and barely three days after the occupation of Makalle, he signalled General de Bono 'to resume the march on Amba Alagi without delay'. This time, de Bono revolted; exasperated beyond measure, he forgot his long-standing loyalty to the Duce and wired back a terse reply, giving him a lesson·in military tactics, 'Note lastly that apart from painful historical memory which, to my thinking, needs no vindication, position of Amba Alagi has no strategical importance and is tactically defective because it can be completely surrounded.' It was the last telegram he was to send as Commander-in-Chief. Six days later, Mus-

apture of Adowa the ponderous talian war machine had halted while e Bono consolidated his position before he embarked on another advance, nd his responses to Mussolini's ignals stressed caution. This so xasperated the Duce, that he finally abled a direct order for the advance o be resumed on the morning of 3rd November and de Bono had no option ut to obey. The next objective was he town of Makale and except for a rush with the Ethiopians on the lopes of Mount Gundi the operation vas uneventful. At dawn on 8th

General Pirzio Biroli, commander of he Eritrean Corps, many of whose Eritrean native troops deserted to the Ethiopians in the first few days

37

Above left : Ethiopian warriors perform a war dance before moving up to the front against the modern artillery, armour and planes of the Italian forces
Left : The news of mobilisation and invasion is beat out in Addis Ababa, and spreads throughout the Empire
Above : Picturesque, but not imposing – swords were to be of little avail against the most powerful invasion force Africa had ever seen

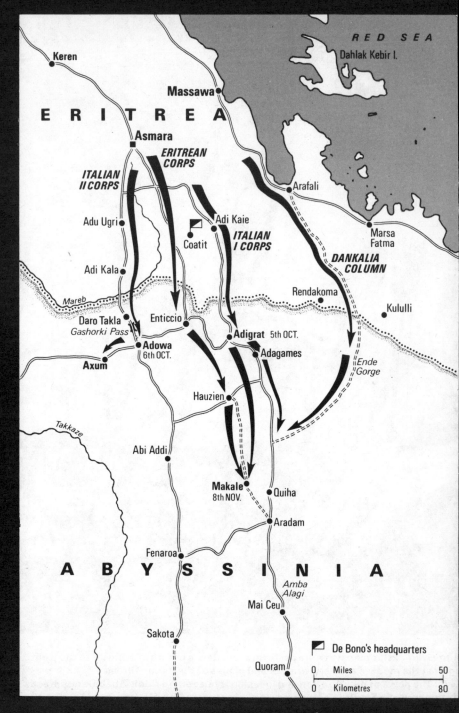

October 1935 : De Bono invades Ethiopia

solini informed him that his task had been completed and that he would be replaced by Badoglio. To sweeten this bitter pill, the Duce promoted him from General to Marshal of Italy.

By substituting Badoglio for de Bono, Mussolini deluded himself into believing that the campaign would be conducted with greater vigour, and would soon be brought to a successful conclusion. In the event the reports submitted to him by Lessona and Badoglio made no mention of the fact that de Bono's halt was essential in order to prepare for the next stage of the campaign. These reports dwelt on the spirit of the troops who were 'panting to push on' and Badoglio wrote that the difficulties were invariably exaggerated and 'that to proceed south was a straightforward tactical problem' which could be solved easily. Solved so easily in fact that Badoglio, who arrived in Eritrea on 20th November 1935, was unable to resume the initiative until 20th January 1936. Political intrigue in Rome had been responsible for de Bono being superseded, and he was not removed because of inefficiency as is generally believed. Badoglio was probably a

Badoglio arrives on the Ethiopian front to take over from de Bono. More impatient and ruthless than his predecessor, he wasted little time before ordering the use of gas

better tactician, but if de Bono had been allowed to stay, it would probably have taken him no longer to reach Addis Ababa than it took Badoglio.

Nevertheless the advent of Badoglio completely altered the character of the war. De Bono, essentially a decent man, had conducted the first phase in a gentlemanly fashion – more in the rôle of pacifier than conqueror. Badoglio, however, had only one aim – to bring the Ethiopian army to battle and wipe it out. And to achieve his purpose, he made use of every weapon he possessed, legal and illegal. De Bono had refused to employ 'special' weapons, whereas Badoglio wasted little time before giving the order to bomb the Ethiopians with mustard and other poison gases. From this point on the war which had begun in the romantic spirit of the *risorgimento* degenerated into a bloody affair of wanton and brutal destruction.

Italian native troops in action as the
Ethiopians begin to resist the invasion

Counter-offensive

One of the main causes of Mussolini's impatience with de Bono was the situation developing at Geneva. On 2nd November 1935 the League had voted to apply economic sanctions to Italy, and the Duce was worried about their effect. Today, most historians agree that they helped rather than hindered the Italian dictator's cause. Because it seemed that Italy was being persecuted by the rest of the world, the Italian people consolidated their home front, and tightened their belts. There were plenty of loopholes in the sanctions, which were not properly enforced anyway – so that they had little effect on the Fascist economy. If the powers responsible for the sanctions had enforced the threatened embargo on oil, and if Britain had closed the Suez Canal to Italian shipping it would have been a very different story. Nevertheless austerity became the order of the day. The Italians were exhorted to eat less meat, use less petrol and electricity,

,nd a 'Buy Italian' campaign was ,aunched. At the same time the ,evelopment of home industries was ,ncouraged, and an intensive drive for ,crap metal was initiated.

Some of the austerity measures were highly unpopular. But the 'harvest of gold' was one ceremony which ,ppealed to the emotional Latins. On 8th December, 1935 several million ,talians took part in a 'rite of faith' to ,hand over their gold wedding rings in ,xchange for rings of steel. Even the Queen of Italy participated in this ,itual, which was designed not just to ,aise money to pay for the war but as a ,pledge of faith in the Fascist regime.

While the Italians were tightening ,heir belts and sacrificing their wed-

'The harvest of gold', 18th December 1935. Millions of Italians, including the Queen, hand over their gold wedding rings in exchange for rings of steel, a ritual designed both to raise money for the war and as a pledge of faith

ding rings, the Ethiopians were counterattacking. Round about the time that Marshal Badoglio assumed command of the Italian expeditionary force, formations of Haile Selassie's numerically immense army had started to march up towards the northern front, then held only by Ras Seyoum Mangasha's force of about 30,000 men. Ras Kassa, the Emperor's second cousin with an army of 40,000 advanced via Dessie towards Makale. A few days behind him came a stronger and better equipped force under the command of Ras Mulugeta. The latter had been a great warrior in his day, and had suppressed a number of revolutions, but he was now over seventy and an alcoholic. Like Kassa, Mulugeta's objective was Makale. Meantime another of the Emperor's cousins, Ras Imru,was moving up from Gojjam with another 40,000 troops towards the River Takkaze.

None of these four men was a military expert. They had been chosen to

command the Emperor's armies for
nepotistic reasons or because Haile
Selassie believed they were loyal to
the throne. None of them had studied
the art of war or undergone any military training in the normally accepted
sense. And, apart from a few young
officers who had graduated from St
Cyr, the Emperor had no one else to
appoint as his generals. Badoglio
contemptuously dismisses the four
rases in his memoirs. But his memoirs
were written a long time after Ras
Kassa and Ras Imru were threatening
to drive him out of Makale. Yet the
plain fact is that for two months in the
winter of 1935, the Ethiopian army
forced the Italians to fall back from
Takkaze to Axum, and from Amba
Tzellene to the Warieu Pass. During
this period the combined action of the
four rases had all the aspects of a
genuine counteroffensive and in Italy

**Rome. Italian troops about to leave for
Ethiopia, now the newest colony**

Ethiopians acclaim their Emperor as he reviews them before they leave for the front

informed circles spoke of these weeks as the 'black period' of the war.

The Italians invariably attributed any success achieved by the Ethiopians to the efforts of white mercenaries in Haile Selassie's pay. Most of these elusive individuals were military advisers and doctors, and although there were never more than a hundred of them the Italian propaganda machine magnified the number to thousands so that the regime could account for the virtual standstill of the Italian army after de Bono's first rapid advance.

A few members of the foreign contingent had lived in Ethiopia before the war; the rest arrived on the eve of the invasion. Many of the latter were opportunists who were hoping to make their fortune without running too many risks, and only a few were men with genuine motives for supporting

While the Italians were tightening their belts and sacrificing their wedding rings, Ethiopian snipers were harassing Badoglio's columns

Haile Selassie's cause. But doctors went to Ethiopia for humanitarian reasons; a Turk, Mehmed Pasha – better known as Wehib Pasha – and an Austrian Dr Schuppler were there because they loathed Mussolini; John Robinson, an American Negro, went to demonstrate the solidarity of the coloured peoples; the rest were anti-fascists, pacifists or philanthropists. Apart from the doctors few made any appreciable contribution. Wehib Pasha, who had been campaigning since 1911, was an exception, and Graziani acknowledged that he was a worthy opponent possessing real military talent.

The largest group of military advisers was made up of Belgians led by Colonel Leopold Ruel. Anxious to avoid giving offence to Italy, the Belgian government had recalled it military mission at the beginning o the war, but raised no objection to the setting up of another composed o volunteers, some of whom had alread seen action in the Congo. Some o these mercenaries were engaged i Paris, and according to *The Mornin Post* (London, 17th September 1935 they were paid 15,000 francs per month with a provision in their contracts fo: their families to receive 50,000 franc as compensation in the event of thei death. Few of them really earned thei pay. But as they were never allowed t take command of Ethiopian troops i action most never had an opportunity to do so. The Ethiopians did not trus them because they were *ferenghi* foreigners, and so their work ofte degenerated into the casual offering o advice, rarely taken; and vague dutie in the way of police work. Ethiopia reluctance to make use of the mer cenaries was due largely to pride. Bu there was also a suspicion that som of them might be spies in the service o Rome. And indeed Colonel Konovalof might well have been an enemy agent By his own account he served Hail Selassie well. Yet it is difficult t rationalise the loyalty of this Whit Russian, who had enjoyed Ethiopia citizenship and the Emperor's favour for more than ten years, with th dedication of his memoirs: 'To th Italian soldier who proved to a scep tical and hostile world that he posses sed the heroic virtues of the Roma legionary, heightened and enhanced b the new climate of Fascism.'

That there were unscrupulous me in the Negus's service there is little doubt. One Frenchman by the name o Drouillet who was sent to Europe t buy an aircraft actually contacted th Italians and offered to abduct Hail Selassie and fly him to Asmara for fee of fifty million lire. Mussolini wa prepared to finance the operation but nothing came of it because a zealous Italian intelligence agent in Paris – ignorant of Rome's negotia tions with Drouillet – succeeded in

48

sequestering Drouillet's new aircraft. Drouillet protested but by the time the plane was freed it was too late to pursue the abduction; Badoglio was already at the gates of Addis Ababa and the project was abandoned.

To compensate for rogues like Drouillet there were men like Count Carl von Rosen of Sweden, who hit the headlines when he took off from Stockholm for Addis Ababa in a plane he had fitted out as a flying ambulance, to offer his services to Haile Selassie. During the war he made flight after flight to evacuate the wounded and take doctors to the areas where they were most needed. Rosen's plane was finally destroyed by the Italian Air Force, who repeatedly attacked it on the landing strip of Quoram despite the fact that the Red Cross was prominently marked on both wings. Then there were the two American negro pilots, John Robinson of Chicago, who flew one of the few Ethiopian planes that were airworthy,

Italian light tanks among the weird cacti of the Ethiopian semi-desert. Ethiopian tactics were simply to swarm *en masse* at the tanks, blocking the machine guns and ripping off the tracks

and Hubert Eustace Julian of Harlem – better known as 'The Black Eagle'. There was also Count Hilaire du Berrier who had made an unsuccessful attempt to raise a company of volunteer pilots in Europe and who was captured by the Italians about fifty miles from Addis Ababa, and the French airmen Corriger, Maillet and Demissie. Lastly, there was the German Weber, who remained in the capital at the risk of his life during the sacking of the city.

All these men made a contribution to the Ethiopian war effort. But the only really worthwhile endeavours made by foreigners proved to be in the field of medicine. And it was only the doctors who suffered for their devotion. Some were treated badly by the

victorious Italians, while others like Melly were to die in the Emperor's service. Theirs is the epic story of a handful of men, short of everything they needed, working ceaselessly under extremely difficult conditions to ease the sufferings of the wounded. The first five field ambulances to make their appearance in Ethiopia after de Bono's men crossed the Mareb, were those of the Ethiopian Red Cross. (Ambulance No 1: Dr Robert W Hockman, of America; No 2: Dr George Dassios, of Greece; No 3: Dr Schuppler, of Austria; No 4: Dr Hooper, of America; No 5: Dr Balau of Poland.) Later, when news of the Italians' indiscriminate bombing reached Europe, the Red Cross sent out more field hospitals. By far the largest of these was that of the British Ambulance Service, under the command of John Melly, which established a field ambulance unit near Lake Ashangi, and another near Goular. Others were provided by the Swedes, and medical teams were sent out to Ethio-pia by the Red Cross of Norway, Finland, Greece and the United States, as well as the Red Crescent organisation of Egypt.

But fifty doctors could do little for an army of half a million men. The world watched from afar but did little else – except offer advice. And plenty of that was transmitted to Addis Ababa. One Englishman wrote suggesting that Ethiopian soldiers should be fitted out with bulletproof waistcoats, which could be obtained quite cheaply. A woman living in New York advised the Negus to adopt the tactics employed by Lawrence of Arabia against the Turks, and sent him an article on the subject by Liddell Hart. An industrialist in Pennsylvania advised Haile Selassie to become a member of the British Commonwealth in order to

The Italian troops, although better armed and equipped, were forced to fall back for two months in the winter of 1935 – for Italy, the 'black period' of the war

Armed with out of date French rifles, a large force leaves Addis Ababa for the northern front under the once redoubtable but now old and alcoholic Ras Mulugeta

gain the immediate armed protection of Great Britain. In addition to letters such as these, there were many from women, both black and white, who wrote to tell Haile Selassie they were praying for him. 'God is full of pity and compassion', ran one these missives. 'Ethiopa must not lose courage, for He will fight on her behalf and send His angels to protect her.' And a negro woman from California wrote: 'I pray that you will deliver yourself from crucifixion and show the whites they are not as civilised as they loudly assert themselves to be . . .'

In December 1935 the Ethiopians in the field felt they had little need of advice from the *ferenghi*. As yet the myth of invincibility had not been destroyed, and the troops that had not yet experienced the aerial might of

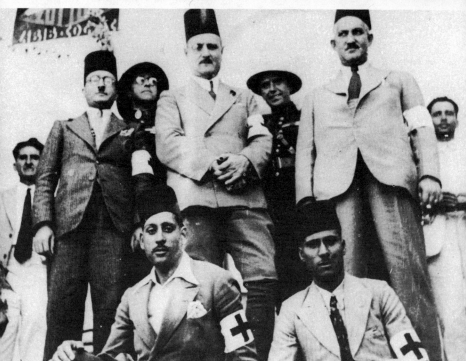

Above left : Poorly armed and often badly led, the Ethiopian casualty rate was high, but the myth of invincibility had not yet been shattered by the Italian air force and the Ethiopians continued to throw themselves into battle with a reckless ferocity
Left : An Egyptian Red Cross unit. In January 1936 it was bombed by the Italians
Above : Ferenghi – foreign military advisers, often regarded with suspicion by the Ethiopians, and attributed by the Italians to be the reason behind the Ethiopian successes

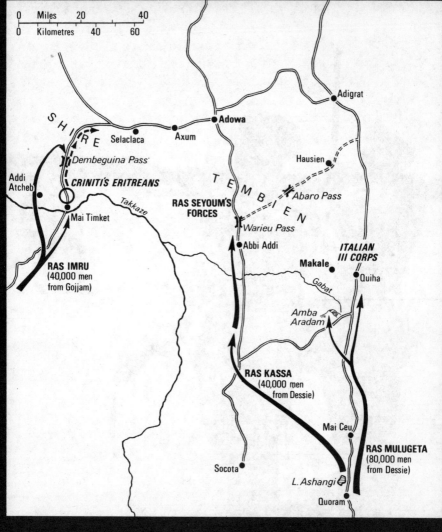

Ethiopian attempts to split the Italian armies

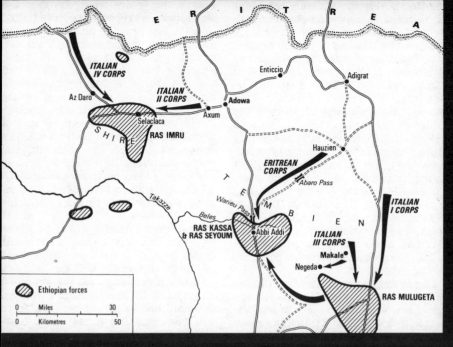

Ethiopian counterattacks are halted

the Regia Aeronautica were confident of victory. At dawn on Sunday 15th December Ras Imru's advance guards crossed the Takkaze by the fords at Mai Tunkat and Addi Atcheb. As one Ethiopian column advanced on Mai Timkat, held by 1,000 Eritrean irregulars, the other column, 2,000 strong, marched rapidly toward the Dembeguina Pass. There it was to cut off the Eritreans commanded by Major Criniti, who promptly withdrew and, protected by nine light tanks, made hurriedly for the pass. This defile was the sole route leading from Shire to the Italian lines at Selaclaca. But when Criniti emerged from the tortuous valley of the Takkaze and reached the plateau, he found Dembeguina already occupied by the Ethiopians.

It was only a few days after Christmas but the sun was at the zenith and the heat was unbearable when the battle began. The Ethiopians were drawn up in a horseshoe formation on the crests of the mountains from Amba Asar to Amba Manamba, when Criniti ordered his tanks to smash a way through them. The tanks lumbered forward but as they approached the Ethiopians, the latter broke ranks and engulfed the steel monsters in a mass of human flesh – preventing the crews from using their machine guns and tearing the tracks off. Criniti ordered his Eritreans to fix bayonets and charge, and he did eventually force a breach through which his force could withdraw. But when dusk fell almost half of his men lay dead or wounded on the battlefield.

The Ethiopians had scored a success – minor in a material sense, but morally of considerable importance. The Italians had been compelled to withdraw for the first time in the campaign, and Ras Imru had gained a position from which to hammer the flanks of Badoglio's army. Badoglio himself was concerned, not so much with the results of this action but with the fact that the initiative seemed to be passing to the Ethiopians along nearly the entire front. In Tembien Ras Kassa was reported to have linked up with Ras Seyoum on the same day as Ras Imru had crossed the Takkaze, and in the Makale sector the vanguard of Ras Mulugheta's force had reached the Geba. Clearly the Ethiopian's aim was to encircle and isolate Makale, and although the Italian Commander-in-Chief was skeptical about the chances of Haile Selassie's generals being able to do this with the resources available to them, he was sufficiently alarmed to wire Mussolini. The Duce, who could not bear to consider a setback, responded with three more divisions and threw one of his Roman rages, during which he spoke of getting rid of Badoglio. In the event Badoglio stayed but one major effect of the Duce's wrath was the decision to use poison gas against the wretched Ethiopians. On 26th December General Graziani had asked for permission to use 'asphyxiating gases', and Mussolini had acquiesced 'when it was considered necessary for supreme defence reasons'. A few days later the Takkaze fords were drenched with mustard gas, and poison gas was dropped on the village of Jijiga (in Graziani's area of operations).

The Ethiopian counter – offensive continued, and a number of bitter hand to hand engagements took place. But gradually it ground to a halt. Italian firepower was sufficient to hold the bravest attacks and the mysterious fluid sprayed from the skies terrified the ignorant Ethiopians; the 'terrible rain that burned and killed' was something that they just could not understand. News that yperite – mustard gas – was being used by the Italians quickly reached the Western world. The Italians first sought to counter the reports which appeared in European newspapers with indignant protests to the effect that the anti-Fascist press was deliberately trying to discredit the Italian army in East Africa. On 30th December 1935 however, Haile Selassie filed a formal complaint with the League of

ations, claiming that Italy's use of poison gas was another violation 'to be added to the long list of the international agreements she has already contravened.'

Faced by a world-wide wave of indignation, the Italian government began strenuously denying that gas had been used and then went on to speak of 'legitimate reprisals' against the Ethiopians who were firing dum-dum bullets and misusing the Red Cross. Finally, a partial admission was made: gas had been employed, but it was not of a lethal type, it merely produced a paralyzing effect which wore off after a few hours. In the meantime, while Rome was rejecting the accusations, the Ethiopians were being systemati-

Top : The Ethiopian air force. When the war began the serviceable part of the force consisted of three tiny and outmoded biplanes. *Above :* As another Ethiopian village is bombed Mussolian's dream of a new Roman Empire comes a little nearer

cally softened up with gas attacks. Having seen the counteroffensive dissolve under the initial attacks, Badoglio and Graziani realized they had a powerful tool with which an Italian victory was assured. In consequence not only was gas used throughout the war, but afterwards as well to break down the resistance of the Ethiopian freedom fighters.

The first battle of Tembien

Spurred on by the ever-impatient
Mussolini, Marshal Badoglio began
the preparations for a renewal of the
Italian offensive. At the height of the
Ethiopian 'Christmas offensive' he
was in a sombre mood. The ignorant
Ethiopians, under the rases whom he
had hitherto regarded as professionally
incompetent, were swarming about the
hills overlooking the Italian positions.
80,000 of Ras Mulugeta's men were
firmly established on the formidable
massif of Amba Aradam, and Badoglio
knew that they would have to be dis-
lodged before he could resume his
southward advance. Mussolini was
bombarding him with the same barrage of orders and instructions as he
had fired at de Bono, and he had made
it clear that he lacked faith in his

Badoglio had appreciated that the main aim of the Ethiopians' plan was to cut the Italian army in two and isolate Makale. While Ras Mulugeta engaged the Italian III Army Coros, Ras Kassa and Ras Seyoum were to force a passage through the Tembien region, occupy the Abaro and Warieu passes, push on to Hauzen, and open up the road for Ras Imru who – after he had retaken Adowa – was to thrust forward into Eritrea. The plan was excellently conceived, but it was on too big a scale, and altogether too ambitious for an army operating on a front of more than 200 kilometres with but a few field radios, limited supplies of ammunition and no air support. By day the Ethiopians were incessantly under attack by the Regia Aeronautica. The sole advantages they had were their extreme mobility and speed, but more often than not they were unable to make use of either because of the heavy ground barrage and constant bombing. To avoid heavy losses they were compelled to proceed with the utmost caution, and Badoglio took good care not to allow them any chance of rushing his positions.

If the Duce had not been prodding him for results it would have been in keeping with Badoglio's nature to wait for the Ethiopians to expend their energies in an attack on his well prepared positions. As it was, he decided to attack – justifying the action in his memoirs as a deliberate move to throw the Ethiopian plan into confusion. On the morning of 19th January General Bastico's III Army Corps left its positions at Makale and occupied Nebri and Negada – so closing the road to Ras Mulugeta and preventing him from sending reinforcements to Rask Kassa. Next day Badoglio launched his Tembien offensive. On the left, the 2nd Eritrean Division advanced in two columns; on the right, a column of

ew commander.

But Badoglio showed no signs of aste. 'It has always been my rule', e cabled Mussolini, 'to be meticulous n preparation so that I may be swift n action.' Before giving the order to dvance, he reinforced his positions, oubled the strength of his artillery, ompleted a network of roads to estab- sh his supply lines and communi- ations, while the Regia Aeronautica ystematically harassed the Ethio- ians with bombs, gas and machine un bullets. Finally at the beginning f January 1936, he was ready to tackle as Mulugeta on Amba Aradam, but ecause of the increasing pressure hat Ras Kassa and Ras Seyoum were xerting in Tembien he was compelled o change his plans.

Blackshirts of the '28th October' Division, which held the Warieu Pass, pushed forward toward the Beles torrent. The Eritreans were stubbornly opposed by the Ethiopians and fierce fighting continued throughout the day. When dusk fell, however, they succeeded in dislodging the Ethiopians from the heights of Zeban Kerkata and the lower slopes of Amba Salama, and Ras Kassa was forced to admit in his radio communiqué to the Negus that the men he had sent to cut off the Italians were now surrounded.

Twenty-four hours later the situation was completely reversed. An Italian force made a sortie from the Warieu garrison, advanced too far, and consequently found itself in imminent danger of being surrounded and wiped out by the troops of Ras Seyoum. The Italians were obliged to fall back, and forced to fight every inch of the way. What remained of this force finally reached the outer defences of the Warieu Pass, but it was not until sunset that the survivors (335 men had been killed or wounded during the retreat) managed to rejoin the garrison. An extremely dangerous situation had arisen: the Ethiopians had succeeded in infiltrating the outer defences and were pushing on towards Zebandas and Dembela on the Adowa road. Worse still, the beleaguered garrison could not expect any help from the 2nd Eritrean Division, which had failed to realize the threatening nature of the enemy's movements and consequently made no move from the positions it had occupied on the previous evening. For three consecutive days the Ethiopians blazed away at the Italians with their rifles, inflicting heavy casualties and forcing the Italians to abandon their peripheral fortifications. As a result Addis Ababa was able to issue a bulletin announcing an authentic victory even though its claims – particularly with regard to the

Ras Imru was unaware that the fighting was going against the Ehtiopians and did not send reinforcements. By the morning of the fifth day Badoglio had won the battle and the Ethiopians were in full retreat

amount of war material captured – were as usual exaggerated.

The siege of the Italians at the Warieu Pass lasted for three days. Ras Kassa, who had been appointed supreme commander of all Ethiopian troops on the northern front, sent an urgent message over his solitary wireless set to Ras Mulugeta, asking him to cooperate in crushing the Italians at Warieu. But Mulugeta, resentful of the fact that Ras Kassa had been promoted over his head, did nothing. Ras Imru, having no radio did not know what was going on in Tembien, and so he too did nothing. Even so, Kassa almost succeeded in over-running the Italian position. Wave after wave of Ethiopians surged forward to assault the Italian fortications and there was a good deal of bloody hand to hand fighting.

Meantime, as the battle raged

20th January. Casualties of the first day of the Tembien offensive

Badoglio had sent two battalions to Warieu to reinforce the hard pressed garrison, and ordered the 1st Eritrean Division to move up to the Abaro Pass to where the 2nd Eritrean Division had withdrawn. The intention was that the latter would also proceed to the Warieu Pass to relieve the beleaguered Italians there. But it would take time to complete this redeployment and the situation in Tembien was critical. On the afternoon of 22nd January when Ras Kassa's attacks were nearing the crescendo of their fury, Badoglio ordered a plan to be prepared for a retirement from Makale. Had such a measure become necessary the repercussions would have been serious for the retreat would have entailed moving some 70,000 men, 14,000 animals and 300 guns down a single road. The operation would have been comparable to Adowa – although Badoglio was probably thinking less of Adowa than of Caporetto, when on 24th October 1917, an Austro-German army had breached his lines at Tolmino and Plezzo and forced the Italians to retreat in disorder all the way back to the Piave. Even though Ras Mulugeta and Ras Imru had failed to come to Kassa's assistance, Kassa's men were fighting with such determination that the possibility of the Italian invasion force being cut in two could not be discounted. Until the relief column, commanded by General Vaccarisi, had reached the Warieu Pass Badoglio was in a state of nervous tension. According to the Italian account Kassa's force melted away when Vaccarisi's troops appeared on the scene. Kassa's version is that his warriors could not stand up to the deadly clouds of mustard gas any longer. During his attacks the routes his men were to take, his base camps and the areas surrounding them were all subjected to an invisible rain of lethal gas.

Thus it was that by the morning of 24th January when the first battle of Tembien came to an end, Kassa's army was in full retreat. Ras Imru was

The IMAM Ro 37bis was the Regia Aeronautica's standard strategic reconnaissance aircraft at the time of the Ethiopian war. The type first appeared in 1934 as a fighter-reconnaissance type, but the quickly advancing state of the art of

still making progress in Shire, but the Ethiopian counter-offensive was over. Badoglio had won the day, while the Ethiopians had suffered 8,000 casualties and almost exhausted their supply of ammunition. Nevertheless the Italians had not got away unscathed. Indeed, though the Ethiopians had had no artillery and no aircraft, the Italian casualties were extremely heavy – sixty officers, 605 Italians and 417 Eritrean askaris killed and wounded. This was the end of another phase of the war, and it left the Italians distinctly uneasy – so much so that Mussolini now began to consider the possibility of a compromise peace. Shukry Yasr Bey, a prominent Palestinian had offered his services as an intermediary and on 24th February 1936 General Roatta flew from Rome to meet Shukry Bey in Athens. In his pocket he carried Mussolini's terms for peace – terms which Haile Selassie could not accept.

Perhaps the greatest effect of the Ethiopian counter offensive was on

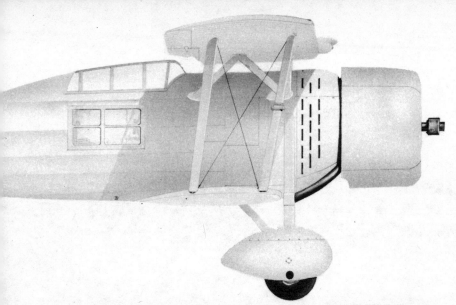

aeronautics in the 30s soon relegated it to the ordinary reconnaissance role. *Engine :* One Piaggio P IX RC 40 or P XR radial, 560- or 700hp. *Speed :* 205mph at 16,400 feet. *Climb :* 9 minutes 20 seconds to 13,120 feet. *Ceiling :* 23,616 feet. *Range :* 696 miles. *Weight empty/loaded :* 3,498/5,335lbs (P IX) or 3,454/5,291lbs (P XR). *Span :* 36 feet $4\frac{1}{8}$ inches. *Length :* 28 feet $1\frac{1}{4}$ inches

the morale of the Italian troops in Badoglio's expedition force. Between December 1934 and January 1936 nearly half a million Italians had disembarked at Massawa and Mogadishu, and because this was the biggest and most varied force in colonial history some comment on its composition is desirable. First, the great majority of the men who were sent to East Africa were conscripts of the 1911 class who had already done their two years compulsory training in Italy. The conscripts outnumbered the regulars by five to one, and despite Mussolini's promise of glory few of them were attracted to the military life. Apart from this, the dread inspired by the unknown, and the reputation of the Ethiopian warriors acquired at Adowa was hardly calculated to raise morale. Africa's wild life, forests and promise of new vistas had little appeal for men whose fathers had told them that the Ethiopian warriors were in the habit of emasculating their prisoners.

But the main source of discord in the expeditionary force was attributable to the uneasy relationship of the conscripts to the Blackshirts. In the army units proper the conscripts had to contend with a discipline far more severe than that to which the Blackshirts were subjected. Moreover the latter usually got better rations and more pay than the conscripts, and this made for bad blood between the regular and so-called volunteer Blackshirt units. Crack units like the Alpini resented the disparity of conditions most bitterly – especially when they bore the brunt of operations and subsequently were compelled to share the honours with the Blackshirts.

Genuine volunteers were few and far between. As boys most of this minority had experienced the exciting atmosphere of the *Balilla* and the *Dux* camps, and when they were old enough had become *squadristi*. Some of them had lived abroad and felt a greater need than the rest for a 'strong' and 'respected' Italy; these were the men

Above: A Savoia-Marchetti SM55. *Below:* Another bomber of the Regia
Aeronautica, an S81. *Right:* A Caproni 113, bombed up and ready to go. Mussolini's
sons, Vittorio and Bruno, flew Capronis, taking part in many of the indiscriminate
bombing raids of the war

who believed they were making history and whom the Italian newspapers eulogized. A few others had offered their services for state, party or dynastic reasons. Mussolini's sons, Vittorio and Bruno, and his son-in-law, Count Ciano – the Minister of Propaganda – were among them. These three arrived in Eritrea as the first preparations for the invasion were being made, with the Capronis of the *Disperata* and *Quia Sum Leo* squadrons, and took part in many of the indiscriminate bombing raids of the war. Subsequently Vittorio, the intellectual member of the Mussolini family, recorded his experiences in the crude and brutal *Flight over the Ambas*. Translated into many languages this authoritative book did more to expose the terrorist activities of the Regia Aeronautica than any other document.

In order to qualify for a share of the expected triumph, various members of the Fascist hierarchy flocked across to Eritrea in the early stages of the war. Among them was Achille Starace, Secretary-General of the Fascist Party, who had always been determined to outshine the rest in Italy and who had made up his mind to be the leading light in Africa. The House of Savoy, which had given its wholehearted blessing to the African undertaking, was also well represented. Princess Marie-Jose of Piedmont went out as a Red Cross nurse, and the Dukes of Bergamo, Aosta, Spoleto and Pistoia all took command of various divisions. Some of these personages remained in Ethiopia until the end of the campaign; some stayed for a few weeks, others just long enough to get a whiff of the war. With them also went a host of journalists, Italian and foreign correspondents, on whose loyalty to the regime the Duce could rely. These writers were to be responsible for chronicling the campaign in exalted terms and after the war almost all of them produced books glorifying the achievement of Italian arms.

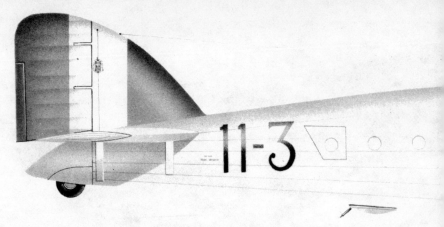

One of the most modern aircraft used by the Italians in Ethiopia, the Savoia-Marchetti SM 81 was used in the bomber, transport, supply and ambulance roles. In the total absence of air opposition, it could roam the skies of Ethiopia at will, the only limiting factors being its range and its reliability, which was high because the Italians had opted for the tri-motor layout at the time when other European nations were adopting two-engined designs. In the long run, the other nations were shown to have exhibited more foresight, but the ruggedness of the SM 81 paid handsome dividends in Ethiopia. Aircraft operating in this theatre, incidentally, often had the upper surfaces of their wings painted with red rays spreading from the inboard areas of the wing leading edges. This was to enable spotter aircraft more easily to spy out machines that had crash-landed in the desert or semi-desert regions of Ethiopia. *Engines :* Three Piaggio PX RC 35 radials, 670hp each. *Armament :* Five 7.7mm machine guns and up to 4,400lbs of bombs (normal bomb load was 2,640lbs). *Crew :* 5. *Speed :* 200mph at 3,280 feet. *Climb :* 25 minutes to 16,400 feet. *Range :* 1,243 miles at 14,750 feet with 4,400lbs of fuel. *Weight empty/loaded :* 14,850/22,176lbs. *Span :* 78¾ feet. *Length :* 60¼ feet

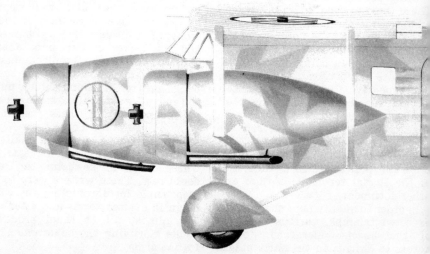

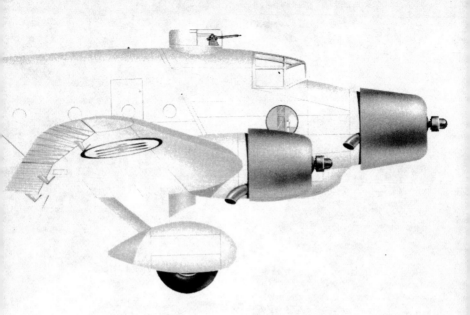

The Caproni Ca 133 was developed in 1934 from the 1931 Ca 101 transport by R Verduzio, who had just joined the Caproni company. It was notable for the extreme aerodynamic cleanness of such parts as the engine cowlings and wheel spats. In service with the Regia Aeronautica, it was used as a bomber and as a troop transport, and was notably successful in the Ethiopian campaign. *Engines* : Three Piaggio

Stella P VII C 16 radials, 460hp each. *Armament :* Four 7.7mm machine guns and a bomb load (under the fuselage) of two 550-lb, one 1,100-lb, six 220-lb or larger numbers of smaller bombs, or eighteen fully-equipped troops in the fuselage. *Speed :* 166mph. *Ceiling :* 18,050 feet. *Range :* 838 miles. *Weight empty/loaded :* 9,420/14,740lbs. *Span :* 69 feet 8 inches. *Length :* 50 feet 4 inches

With Graziani to Neghelli

General Rudolfo Graziani was a ruth- less and ambitious man, quoted as once saying that 'the Duce shall have Ethiopia, with or without the Ethio- pians'. No doubt he meant what he said: that he would have been pre- pared to liquidate the whole popu- lation of Ethiopia if they stood in the way of the Italian conquest. In Libya he had suppressed a Senussi revolt with singular brutality and set up concentration camps and 'flying tri- bunals' to administer swift justice to any Libyan subject who dared question Italy's authority.

Graziani landed at Mogadishu on 7th March 1935 in a disagreeable mood. In his view the decisive battles would be fought in the north, where the Ethiopians had concentrated most of their forces. Nearly the whole of the Italian expeditionary force had been assembled on the Eritrean border and it appeared that he had been relegated to a secondary front, where his rôle would be purely defensive. Only one Italian division, the Peloritana, had been allotted to the southern front, while de Bono had ten. Moreover his orders were to dig in and wait for the Ethiopians to attack. To a man as ambitious and as resentful as Graziani, this was less than he deserved, and he set out to convince Mussolini that the

plans for the campaign needed to be modified in order to permit the army in the south to play a more active rôle. The Duce was more than ready to listen; he wanted action – which was what Graziani promised. In con- sequence Graziani's preparations for an offensive had tacit approval from Rome, if not from de Bono, and later Badoglio.

Between April and December 1935 Graziani opened up new roads, de- veloped the port facilities at Moga- dishu, solved the difficult problem of water supply, stocked up the provisions and munitions he would need for an offensive, and bought hundreds of motor vehicles (most of these provided by American manufacturers) from British car dealers in Mombasa and Dar-es-Salaam. By the time war broke out Graziani had sufficient equipment and supplies for a march on Harar. He had also cultivated the support of certain Somali chiefs who had no love for the Ethiopians. (With arms provided by the Italians their followers had been waging a guerilla war against the Ethiopians since 1933.)

When the war began, Graziani was confronted by an enemy 80,000 strong. Of these, 40,000 under the command of Ras Desta Damtu were massed in the provinces of Sidamo and Bale, 30,000 commanded by Ras Nasibu held the fortified towns of the Ogaden and Harar and manned a defence line organised by Wahib Pasha; while the remaining 10,000 were concentrating

Their land occupied by the invaders, local inhabitants establish amicable relations with an Italian divisional commander

in Arussi. The two principal armies on the southern front were better trained and equipped than those in the north, and their commanders were young, progressive and loyal individuals dedicated to Haile Selassie's cause. As such they were very different from the four rases commanding the armies in the north. Ras Desta was the emperor's son-in-law, while Ras Nasibu, who had travelled extensively abroad, was regarded by the Negus as one of the most promising of his entourage.

On 3rd October, when de Bono crossed the Mareb, Graziani activated his 'Milan Plan' – the object of which was to eliminate the Ethiopian frontier posts and test the Ethiopian reactions to a series of probes all along the southern front. These preliminary operations were hindered by incessant rains. But within three weeks the frontier villages of Callafo, Dagnerai, Gerlogubi and Gorahai had been occupied. Gorahai – the most important of these – had been turned into an armed camp by the redoutable *Gerazmatch* (literally 'Commander of the Left-Wing' – a rank corresponding to colonel or brigadier) Afewerk, who was posthumously pro-

moted to the rank of *Dejazmatch* (General) by the Negus. Capronis of the Regia Aeronautica repeatedly bombed Gorahai and Afewerk himself directed the fire of the only anti-aircraft gun in the village – an Oerlikon 37mm, mounted on top of one of the turrets of the Mad Mullah's old fort. During one of these raids Afewerk was wounded, but he refused to be taken to hospital because he knew that the morale of his men would suffer. Within forty-eight hours the wound became gangrenous and Afewerk collapsed and died. As he had feared the remaining defenders then fled in panic.

Having occupied Gorahai, Graziani sent a flying column under Colonel Maletti in pursuit of Afewerk's force. Maletti caught up with the Ethiopians about fifty miles from the frontier, where they had halted and dug into await the Italians. Battle was joined on the dry soil under a pitilessly hot sun, and fighting continued for some hours. At the end of it both sides had suffered heavy losses, and both withdrew claiming victory. By rights the Italians should have won, if only because of their vastly superior equipment. But in this engagement the light tanks on which they relied for supporting fire were bogged down in treacherous terrain, and were quickly knocked out of action by Ethiopians who crept up and fired into the weapon slits in the armour.

The initiative now passed to the Ethiopians, just as it had passed to them on the northern front. In order to relieve the pressure on Harar, Ras Desta left the Bale plateau, assembled his army at Neghelli and advanced towards Dolo in three columns, with the obvious intention of invading Italian Somaliland. But his plan was too ambitious. Apart from the fact that there was nothing novel about it – and like all Ethiopian man-oeuvres was the talk of the market-place – it did not take into account the distance the army would have to march from Dolo to Neghelli (over 200 miles), the difficulty of supplying such a large force en route, and the devastating effects of attacks by the Regia Aeronautica. Indeed, although they only moved at night the ill-concealed Ethiopians were soon spotted by Graziani's reconnaissance planes, and subjected to incessant bombing. By the time Ras Desta's army reached the first Italian outposts on the Somali frontier the fire had completely gone from its belly. The combination of air attacks, the long march through the pitiless desert, meagre rations, dysentry and malaria, shattered its morale. And Ras Desta, realizing it would be useless to think of assaulting the Italian positions,

71

The modern mechanised Italian army
continues its advance against a
backward people

Italian askaris, well equipped and well trained

The southern front. Graziani's troops
push over the border, meeting little
resistance

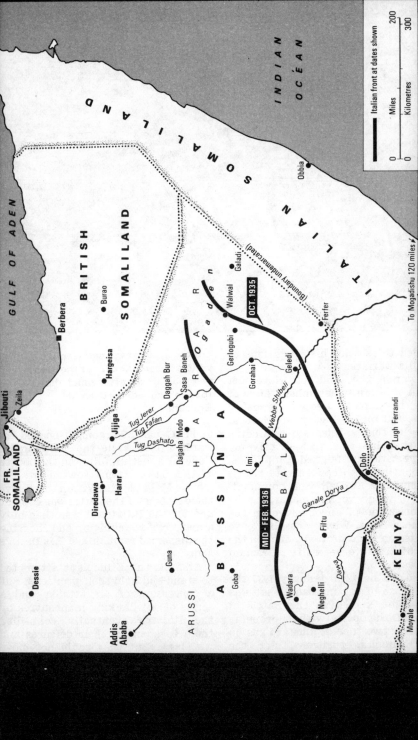

GULF OF ADEN

INDIAN OCEAN

FR. SOMALILAND

BRITISH SOMALILAND

ITALIAN SOMALILAND

Jibouti
Zeila
Berbera
Burao
Hargeisa

Daggah Bur
Sasa Baneh
Tug Jerer
Tug Fafan
Jijiga

Dagaha Modo
Tug Dashato

Harar
Diredawa

OGADEN

HARAR

Gerlogubi
Gorahai
Geledi
Walwal
Galadi

Webbe Shibeli

Imi

BALE

ABYSSINIA

Guna
Goba
ARUSSI

Dessie

Addis Ababa

MID – FEB. 1936

OCT. 1935

Ferfer

(Boundary undemarcated)

Lugh Ferrandi

Dolo

Ganale Dorya

Filtu

Wadara
Neghelli

Daw'a

KENYA

Moyale

Obbia

To Mogadishu 120 miles

Italian front at dates shown

Miles
Kilometres

0   200   300

decided to restrict his operations to guerilla warfare.

Towards the end of November Graziani began to assemble a force at Dolo to attack Desta's famished horde. But on 7th December, Marshal Badoglio sent a telegram reminding him that his rôle was strictly defensive. Graziani feigned compliance, but continued to concentrate troops and supplies at Dolo and communicated privately with Rome, urging the authorisation of an offensive on the southern front. When Mussolini gave permission for 'a limited attack in the case of absolute necessity', Graziani was ready.

At dawn on 12th January 1936 the first phase of the massacre that was to become known as the Battle of Ganale Doria opened with the dropping of nearly two tons of mustard gas on the Ethiopian positions. For the ground operation Graziani had split his force into three columns. The first, under General di Popolo advanced up the valley of the Ganale Doria towards Bardia; the second

Ethiopian dead at the massacre which became known as the battle of Ganale Doria, after which the road to Neghelli lay open for Graziani

under General Bergonzoli headed towards Filtu; while the third, under General Agostini, followed the course of the Dawa Parma towards its objective Malka Muin. Within three days the outcome of the battle was evident and for the Italians it was then only a matter of rounding up and shooting the dispersed remnants of Ras Desta's army.

At first, the Ethiopians attempted to stand and hold their positions. But a succession of air attacks and a series of out-flanking manoeuvres by the Italians eventually compelled them to abandon their defences and withdraw. But they could not move fast enough and what set out to be an orderly withdrawal quickly turned into a tragic retreat. Pursued by mechanized columns through camel-thorn bush and across burning sand

he wretched Ethiopians were pre-
ented from approaching the few wells
hat lay along their route. Parched
ith thirst, they sought desperately
o escape the inexorable dragnet and
each the rivers. But those who had
ot collapsed during the terrible
etreat were mowed down by machine
uns almost as soon as they reached
he river banks. All Desta's men could
hink about was their crying need for
ater, and they were shot down like a
orde of wild animals. And when
esta's army no longer existed, the
oad to Neghelli lay open. It took the
hree columns five days to converge
n this capital of Galla Borana, but
hey occupied it on 20th January
ithout a shot being fired. As almost
orty tons of bombs had been dropped
n Neghelli, and the inhabitants had
aken to the bush, this was hardly
urprising.

Graziani's tactics showed a certain
mount of intelligent foresight. But
need hardly be said that he owed
uch of his success to superior

organisation and administration and
to the Capronis of the Regia Aeronautica. Moreover there was one event
which detracted from his triumph and
which rankled in his mind for a long
time afterwards. Halfway through the
battle over nine hundred of his Eritrean askaris had deserted. Some made
their way to Kenya, others eventually
joined what remained of Ras Desta's
army. By an odd coincidence a number
of askaris deserted on the northern
front a few days later. At the end of a
fierce day's fighting *Shumbashi* Andoru
Tesfazien was ordered to bury the
Italian dead and leave the Eritreans
where they had fallen. Filled with
indignation Tesfazien insisted that as
the Eritreans had fought side by side
with the Italians they had an equal
right to a grave. Sentenced to punishment for insubordination, Tesfazien
went over to the Ethiopians with a
hundred of his men. Other Eritreans
followed, and on the eve of the battle
of Mai Ceu Tesfazien's band was
reported to be over a thousand strong.

The decisive battles

On 9th February 1936 Marshal Badog
held a press conference at his hea
quarters, and announced that he w
going to liquidate the mighty obsta
that blocked the road to Addis Aba
He was speaking of Ras Muluget
army and the great mountain of Am
Aradam on which it was firmly e
sconced. Amba Aradam, with its roc
precipitous sides and level summit
a natural fortress, somewhat rer
niscent of that other strongho
Masada, on whose heights the Je
fought to the last man in a bloo
battle against the Romans. Badog
did not relish the task of assaulti
it. Since the Ethiopian offensive h
fizzled out, he had gained confider

nd he had reorganised his front and assembled the biggest and most powerful expeditionary force ever to have taken part in a colonial war. Numerically he was about on a par with his enemy – although the Italian press had followed their usual customary procedure of exaggerating the Ethiopian strength as a precautionary measure. So far as firepower was concerned the Italians with more than 0,000 machine guns, 280 pieces of artillery and 170 planes, were in a completely different class from that of Mulugeta's men who could muster only 400 machine guns, 18 old guns of medium calibre, and a few anti-aircraft Oerlikons. Moreover the Regia Aeronautica had thoroughly mapped the Amba Aradam region and air photographs showed that its defences could be penetrated from the plain of Antalo in the rear. Mulugeta had disposed his troops to defend the mountain's impregnable northern wall and its virtually impregnable east and west faces. He was not expecting an attack from the south, and for some weeks his men had been sheltering from the Italian bombers

An Italian column *en route* for the major obstacle on the road to Addis Ababa – the mountain of Amba Aradam, on which Ras Mulugeta's army was firmly lodged

in the caves with which the mountain was riddled.

Before dawn on 10th February, the strong Italian I and III Army Corps started to advance across the undulating Calamino Plain, and by the evening they were established on the left bank of the river Gabat. When they resumed their march in torrential rain the following morning, then he reacted with a furious attack on the Blackshirt '3rd January' Division on the slopes of Ender Gaber. The Blackshirts were held up, but the Alpini of the Pusteria Division struck out on a wider encirclement and continued on towards the objective of Antallo. The Ethiopians made no attempt to block the move of the Alpini, and it was apparent that there

Italian askari dead after the battle of Amba Aradam. By 19th February Ras Mulugeta's army was routed, and he himself was soon to be killed

the Ethiopians had not given any signs of life. Not until the afternoon of 12th February did Mulugeta appear to realise that the Italians were executing an encircling movement. But was little, if any, direction of their resistence. The fact was that old Mulugeta had been stunned by the continuous and persistent bombardment of Badoglio's guns and aircraft which had also sapped the morale of his troops.

This was the sort of battle that was suited to Badoglio's taste—the swift and effective business of a modern industrial nation, a war of annihilation designed to prove once and for all that the Italians were entitled to their slice of the African cake and that they were not going to waste time getting it.

The Italian pincers were ready to snap shut by the evening of 14th February. The encircling columns had reached their forming up places, re-

grouped, and moved up their artillery ready for the assault. For two days the Ethiopians had done little to prevent the Italians completing their arrangements, although when they did attack in the traditional Ethiopian manner – charging *en masse* – the sight of cold steel usually resulted in the Italians giving way.

Some 250 miles to the south, at Dessie, Haile Selassie was vainly attempting to coordinate the actions of his four armies on the northern front. On the morning of 12th February, after talking to Mulugeta on the radiotelephone, he sent a telegram to Ras Kassa ordering the latter to go to Mulugeta's aid. If he attacked Badoglio's flanks, the Negus said, the Italians would fall back and the pressure on Mulugeta would be relieved. This plan had a good deal of merit, but for some mysterious reason the telegram did not reach Kassa until the evening of 15th February – by which time Mulugeta had decided it was impossible to defend Amba Aradam and had ordered his troops to retire to the mountain passes of Amba Alagi. Meantime Ras Imru, who had no radio, was continuing his slow advance towards the Mareb.

Near Amba Aradam the battle was approaching its bloody climax. The Italians completed their encirclement of the mountain fortress in the early morning of 15th February under the cover of darkness and dense cloud. When daylight came and the cloud base lifted the Ethiopians saw the danger they were in clearly for the first time. Swarming down the western slopes of their mountain fortress towards Addi Kolo they attacked the Italians at the foot of Amba Aradam repeatedly. But their furious onslaughts were checked by the concentrated barrage laid down by Badoglio's artillery and the bombs of his aircraft. Proximity to the air strip at Makale enabled the Regia Aeronautica to keep at least a dozen aircraft in the air over the battlefield throughout the day. (This was the forerunner of the cab-rank technique developed and used so successfully by both sides between 1940 and 1945.)

When darkness settled over the scene the battle was practically over. The Italian pincers had not snapped shut because the attacks round Addi Kolo had prevented the I and II Army Corps from linking up. This left a gap through which the Ethiopians were

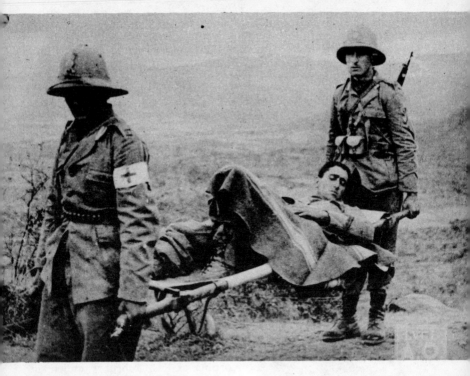

The Italians suffered some 800
casualties in all, as against 6,000
Ethiopians killed and nearly twice that
number wounded

able to fall back towards Amba Alagi
and Sokota. But the fall of Amba
Aradam was now assured. All that
remained to defend it were the few
hundred men who had been ordered to
cover the retreat of the rest of Mulugeta's disorganised army. The task of
liquidating this rearguard fell to the
Alpini, but for political reasons the
honour of hoisting the Italian flag on
Amba Aradam was given to the Blackshirts of the '23rd March' Division.
Naturally enough this did nothing
towards improving the relations between the conscripts and the Blackshirt volunteers.

Meantime Badoglio ordered the
assaulting columns to halt, and the
task of exploiting his success was left
to the Regia Aeronautica. Pursuit of
a beaten enemy – traditionally the
rôle of a cavalry force hitherto – was a

novel commitment for the air forc
but they took to it with gusto. An
for four consecutive days every singl
plane on the northern front took par
in the bombing of the hapless fugitive
from Amba Aradam. By moder:
standards the aerial charges made b:
the Italian bombers and fighter
would be considered a puny effort
But forty tons of high explosive wer
dropped on Mulugeta's columns an
to people who had rarely seen a:
aircraft before, the effect was devast
ating. To add to the horror of th
bombing came the terror of th
Azebu Galla. This treacherous tribe
who hated their Shoan overlords, ha
become an easy prey to Italian cor
ruption, and they had been armed an
paid by Badoglio's agents in readines
for this very day. As the fugitive
retreated, they were constantly har
assed and ambushed by the Gallas
and thrown into confusion. Ra
Mulugeta's son was in command of th
rearguard, and in one of the desperat
little actions with the Galla he wa

killed and mutilated. When the news of this reached Mulugeta, the old ras turned back to avenge his son. En route his party was spotted by a low-flying plane which strafed the area and Mulugeta was mortally wounded. This was the last event of note, and on 19th February the battle for Amba Aradam – or Enderta, as it was to become known – officially came to an end. The Italians had suffered some 800 casualties in all, as against over 6,000 Ethiopians killed and nearly twice that number wounded.

Having dealt with Ras Mulugeta, Badolglio turned on the armies of Ras Kassa and Ras Seyoum; that of Ras Imru, which had taken up a defensive position in Shire, he decided to leave to another day. By this time the extra divisions he had asked Mussolini for had arrived in Eritrea and the network of roads guaranteeing his supplies had all but been completed. In the field the total strength of the armies of the three rases totalled about 60,000, while Badoglio could call on a total of three times that number. Even so, the Italian commander was not prepared to undertake anything rash, and before any move was made to attack Ras Kassa and Ras Seyoum in Tembien, 48,000 shells and 7 million rounds of small arm ammunition had been dumped in the forward areas.

Badoglio's plan was to send the III Army Corps towards Gaela to cut off Ras Kassa's main line of withdrawal. When it was established across the roads running south from the Abbi Addi region, the Eritrean Corps would advance south from the Warieu and Abaro passes; Kassa and Seyoum would then be in the jaws of a great trap. When Kassa sent a wireless message to the Negus asking for permission to withdraw from Tembien, it seemed that he had sensed Badoglio's intention. (In effect this request was superfluous as Haile Selassie had already told him that he should fall back on Amba Alagi and link up with what remained of Mulugeta's depleted force.) But something caused Kassa to change his mind, and on the morning of 27th February when the Eritrean Corps came down from the mountains and the III Army Corps moved up from the Geba valley, the armies of Kassa and Seyoum were drawn up in battle array in front of Abbi Addi.

The second battle of Tembien was fought in terrain which favoured the defence – in a region of forests and ravines and torrents, where the Italians were unable to deploy their artillery properly or use their armoured vehicles. But Ras Seyoum's warriors failed to take advantage of this fact and so were defeated. The right flank of the Ethiopian armies rested on Amba Work, the 'mountain of gold' on which the Ethiopians had established a strong point. Because Amba Work blocked the road to Abbi Addi on which Badoglio's III Corps and the Eritrean Corps were to converge it was vital ground, and 150 Alpini and Blackshirts commandos were ordered to capture it under cover of darkness. Armed with grenades and knives, they found the Ethiopians asleep on the summit when they scaled the peak and the issue was settled in a matter of minutes.

Once Amba Work was in Italian hands, two columns from the Eritrean Corps set off towards Zebandas and Worrega, and the inevitable clash came early on the morning of 27th February. Heralded by a wail of battle horns and the roll of the *negarait,* the war drum, a seemingly uncoordinated mass of Ethiopians left the cover of the woods covering the slopes of Debra Ansa to fling themselves at the Italians. From 8am until 4pm, wave after wave of Ethiopian warriors, armed for the most part only with swords and clubs, tried to break through or get round the forward lines established by the Alpini and Blackshirts of the Eritrean columns. Time and time again the waves were mowed down and turned back by the concentrated machine

48,000 shells and 7,000,000 rounds of small arms ammunition are brought up for the second battle of Tembien

gun fire of the Italians. Finally, when the attacks seemed to be less frequent and less fanatic, General Pirzio Birolli, the Italian commander, counterattacked. Pounded by artillery, hounded by the bombers that had dropped nearly 200 tons of high explosive on their forming up zones, and now threatened with encirclement from Birolli's advancing infantry, Ras Seyoum's warriors decided they could take no more punishment. When they fled from the battlefield they left more than a thousand dead.

With his right flank in the air Ras Seyoum ordered his army to pull back to the Takkaze fords. But as his men straggled back along the one road open to them they were bombed repeatedly, and the rocky ravine where they were to cross the river turned out to be a bottleneck. To the Italian aviators the solid mass of defeated Ethiopians was a bomber's dream, and the area round the fords was soon turned into a charnel house.

Meanwhile Ras Kassa on Debra Amba, whose troops had not yet been in action, had decided to follow the Negus's orders and withdraw from Tembien. Now it was his turn to be bombed as he fell back towards the Geba. The Eritrean Corps linked up with III Corps at noon on 29th February about three miles west of Addi Abbi. By this time, however, despite the attacking from the air, some 200,000 men of the armies of Ras Kassa and Ras Seyoum had escaped Badoglio's dragnet. But they were demoralised and their fighting days were over. All the men could think about was getting away from the region – away from the bombs and the mustard-gas, and the deadly rattle of machine gun fire. And as the two armies moved south desertions thinned their ranks. Thus, when Kassa and Seyoum reached Haile Selassie's headquarters at Quorom after two weeks of forced marches, they were accompanied by little more than their personal bodyguards.

The Ethiopian armies were now beginning to disintegrate, and Haile Selassie was well aware of the gravity of the situation. To Ras Imru, the only commander on the northern front who had not suffered defeat, he wrote 'Our army, famous throughout Europe for its valour, has lost its name; brought to ruin by a few traitors; to this pass it is reduced ... those who were the first to betray us, and those who followed their example, namely the chiefs of the Wollo forces ... have all been arrested . . . Ras Kassa and Ras Seyoum are with us, but have not a single armed man with them . . .' In conclusion, he asked Ras Imru to 'come and die with us' in the battle he was determined to fight against the Italians, the battle that was to lead to the final defeat of the Ethiopians on the northern front. It was the tragic letter of a desperate man, a man who had held out for five months against an enemy infinitely more powerful than himself in the hope that the League of Nations would come to his aid – a man who now found himself betrayed by his own chiefs who went over to the Italians for money, or left him to his fate because they had been his rivals. This letter is the key to the battle of Mai Ceu, the battle which should never have been fought, but which the Negus insisted on commanding in person because he knew it was his only hope of retaining the shreds of his remaining prestige.

By the evening of 29th February the Italians had completed their encircling manoeuvre and the second battle of Tembien was virtually over. The few thousand Ethiopians who were trapped put up a desperate resistance which roused even Badoglio's admiration. But they could do nothing to change the course of events which had overtaken them. When the

Eritrean askari machine gunners in the second battle of Tembien

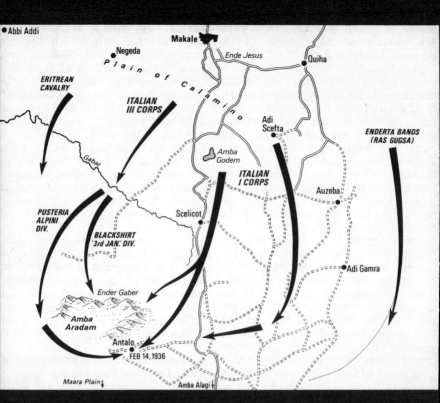

The fall of Amba Aradam

casualties were totted up the Ethiopians had lost some 8,000 killed for less than 600 Italians and Eritreans killed or wounded.

News of this victory, together with an announcement that I Army Corps had occupied Amba Alagi was received in Italy with the same frenzied delight that had characterized the news that Adowa had been taken. 1st March was the fortieth anniversary of the defeat at Adowa and the coincidence of the victories provided Mussolini's propaganda machine with some first-class material. (In fact the coincidence was not exactly unexpected, as the Duce had told Badoglio that he would be replaced by Graziani unless he effected some glittering coup.) Thanks to the Fascist regime the dead of Adowa had at last been revenged.

Paradoxically, the fortieth anniversary of Adowa was also being celebrated in Addis Ababa, despite the shattering defeats inflicted in Tembien. And in Europe Hitler was preparing to re-occupy the Rhineland, and take the first step in the series of territorial grabs that was to lead to the Second World War. Seven days later, when the Wehrmacht crossed the Rhineland frontier, the alarm bells rang in every chancellery of Europe and Mussolini's adventure in Ethiopia became a secondary consideration. From here on it was a short step for the League of Nations to more or less abandon Haile Selassie to his fate.

By the end of February two of the Ethiopian armies had been virtually wiped out, and on the northern front there was only Ras Imru's force to be reckoned with. Badoglio was now set on taking Imru by surprise and annihilating his army in the last of the great battles in Tigre. To do this he brought up General Maravigna's I Army Corps, and General Babbini's IV Army Corps. This brought the force he could deploy to a strength of 37,000 men – twice the strength of the Ethiopian force it was to annihilate. Meantime, after Ras Kassa's defeat, Ras Imru had decided to withdraw from Shire before the Italians could trap him. The main body of his army began to retire towards the Takkaze and positions were taken up on the heights of Semanca, Addi Hainmanal and Selaclaca to cover the withdrawal. Badoglio knew little of Imru's dispositions, and his plan was for II Corps to advance from Axum and attack Imru in the area where he was known to be operating, about thirty miles from the town. At the same time IV Corps would move south from the Eritrean border, across unknown and very difficult terrain, to attack Imru's left flank. If only because of the lack of roads and tracks manoeuvre was extremely hazardous, and it was accomplished successfully only by virtue of the superhuman efforts and achievements of the Italian supply system. General Fidenzio Dall'Ora, who had already proved his worth in the build-up of the original expeditionary force now showed his superb ability by wringing a staggering amount of supplies out of the port of Massawa.

Maravigna's force of 20,000 men left Axum and began their advance towards Selaclaca at dawn on 29th February. As the terrain was fairly open, and no Ethiopian troops had been reported to be anywhere in the area, Maravigna had decided to forego security for speed. The only existing road which could be used by motor vehicles constituted the axis of his advance, and his force was soon strung out along this route. The Blackshirt '21st April' Division headed the long column; behind it came the Gavinana, the Gran Sasso, the 2nd Eritrean Brigade with a few detachments of cavalry functioning as a very casual flankguard. All went well until midday. But – as often happens when risks of this nature are taken – the unforeseen was bound to occur, and Maravigna's troops were soon to pay for their commander's rashness. When the column reached a crest overlooking the Selaclacla plain the 'Gavinana' moved up to take the lead

Italian tanks move up, virtually
unopposed

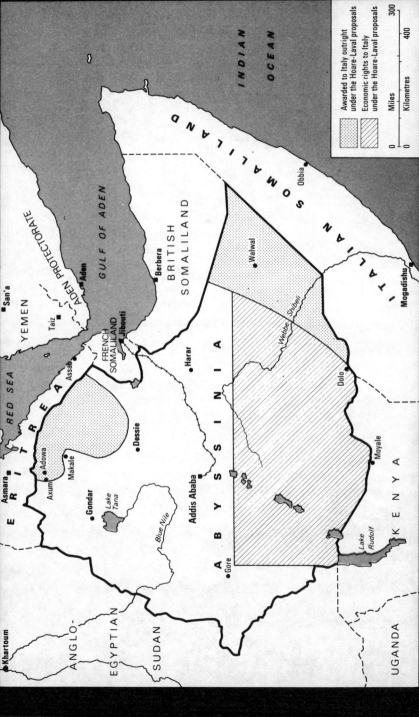

INDIAN OCEAN

RED SEA

GULF OF ADEN

Awarded to Italy outright
under the Hoare-Laval proposals

Economic rights to Italy
under the Hoare-Laval proposals

Miles 0 300
Kilometres 0 400

YEMEN
San'a
Taiz
Aden
ADEN PROTECTORATE

ERITREA
Asmara
Adowa
Axum
Makale
Gondar
Lake Tana
Blue Nile
Dessie

ABYSSINIA
Addis Ababa
Gore
Harar

Khartoum
ANGLO-EGYPTIAN SUDAN

UGANDA

KENYA
Moyale
Lake Rudolf

FRENCH SOMALILAND
Jibouti
Assab

BRITISH SOMALILAND
Berbera

Walwal

Webbe Shibeli
Dolo

ITALIAN SOMALILAND
Obbia
Mogadishu

rom the '21st April'. But it had barely esumed the advance when it was uddenly caught in a deadly cross-fire. The column had driven straight into n ambush, and the battle that ensued asted for ten hours. Covered by the re from machine guns hidden in the ush, the Ethiopians threw themselves n the Italians. All the latter could do as to form a series of squares, and he artillery they had with them was irtually useless. This was the sort f engagement to which the Italians ere as ill suited as the Ethiopians ere well fitted, and for a time it was ouch and go whether or not the avinana's ammunition trucks would e captured.

Shaken by this engagement nd overestimating the Ethiopian trength, Maravigna called off the dvance, ordered a defensive position o be formed and the men to dig in. adoglio was furious at the post-onement of his operation, and Ras nru was given an extra forty-eight ours to continue his orderly with-rawal to the Takkaze. Maravigna's en resumed their advance on 2nd larch but they made little progress gain that day because they ran into nru's rear-guard. The Ethiopians ught with fanatical fury, and as sual the Italians stopped to bring o bear the weight of their artillery nd the power of the Regia Aero-autica.

But when dawn broke on 3rd March he Ethiopians had gone. During the ight they had broken off the action nd slipped away, leaving Maravigna a complete void. Meantime the alian IV Corps, which by this time ould have been threatening the left ank and rear of Ras Imru's army, was ill about five miles away at Az Daro. he two corps had failed to close the ap, and the last few hundred thiopians covering the withdrawal d themselves in caves and had to be riven out one by one. For the Italians e battle of Shire was the toughest ey had fought. When it was over, Corps had suffered nearly 1,000

casualties of whom only twelve were Eritreans. The Ethiopians left 4,000 killed or wounded on the battlefield; for the first time, their losses were a mere four to one – and not the usual ten to one ratio.

But the battle was not yet over, and the Ethiopian casualties were soon to rise to the usual dispropportionate figure. As Ras Imru's main body had gone away, and neither the II or IV Corps were either fit or ready to pursue the Ethiopians, Badoglio ordered the Regia Aeronautica to take up the chase and smash the flying enemy with every means at their disposal. On 3rd March and 4th bombers zoomed over Ras Imru's army at the Takkaze fords and dropped eighty tons of high explosive and incendiary bombs on the columns of Ethiopians struggling across the river. Beyond the river and up the wooded slopes of the Takkaze valley other bombers sprayed the deadly mustard gas, while Badoglio's fighters roared in at ground level to machine-gun those who had survived the bombs. When Maravigna's men crossed the same fords a few days later thousands of putrefying corpses testified to the effectiveness of the Italian air arm.

Ras Imru himself had escaped death, and had managed to get about 10,000 of his men across the river. But most of them were completely demoralized, and as soon as the opportunity was presented they slipped away to return to their homes. By the time Imru reached Delva Markos desertions and persistent air attacks on his column had thinned the ranks of his army to the 300 men of his personal body-guard. With the attention of the Regia Aeronautica compelling him to move by night Imru made slow pro-gress, and twice he escaped capture by the Italians only by a hair's breadth. It took him a month to reach Debra Markos and when he did arrive it was only to learn that Haile Selassie had left Addis Ababa for Jibouti, and that the Italians were about to occupy the capital. At this point Imru,

realizing the hopelessness of the situation, started to recruit a new army to continue the struggle in guerilla activity.

With Ras Imru's force routed, only Haile Selassie's one other army stood in Badoglio's path to Addis Ababa and prevented him over running the rest of Ethiopia. During March, therefore, when the I Army Corps pushed on beyond the Alagi Passes to Mai Ceu, the Italian Commander-in-Chief occupied the whole of the northern regions now open and virtually undefended. He also sent a number of independent motorised columns to occupy Gondar, Debarah, Sokota and Sardo. These operations were carried out systematically and as there was little opposition they were concluded quickly. At the same time Badoglio prepared for the next advance of his main force. A network of roads was constructed; supplies were dumped in the forward area; two lines of forts were created to protect the main lines of communication; bands of Azebu Galla were armed, paid and organised to patrol the conquered areas, and the main force was redeployed in readiness for the coming offensive.

The stage was set for the final drama. Except for the force at Mai Ceu commanded in person by Haile Selassie – an army completely loyal and still intact – the Ethiopians were defeated. The Negus's treasury was empty and there were no arms with which to re-equip the demoralized remnants of the four other armies which had originally faced the Italians on the northern front. At Geneva the League of Nations had so little interest left in Ethiopia that it did not even take the trouble to study the proposals for a negotiated peace put forward by its Committee of Thirteen, but allowed them to founder. The League 'noted' and 'deplored' the

Italian flamethrowers, yet another modern weapon which eroded the Ethiopians' morale

The castle of Gondar. Its medieval serenity was shattered by the arrival of one of Badoglio's columns after the Italians had won at Tembien

fascist act of aggression, but accepted Italy's *fait accompli* and – even worse – its own impotence. Haile Selassie no longer had any hope of salvation by the League.

In Rome it seemed that the clouds had lifted. Italians who had been preoccupied with anxiety for their expeditionary force and a dread that their country might find itself at war with Britain, breathed more freely. In northern Ethiopia Badoglio also breathed more freely. Up to this time he had been concerned about Haile Selassie's intentions, and worried that the Negus would prefer guerilla warfare to giving battle. While an organised Ethiopian army remained Badoglio's task was unfulfilled. If Haile Selassie retreated, the Italian supply line would have to be lengthened and precious weeks would be lost. The rainy season was almost due and instead of bringing the war to a triumphant conclusion within a couple of months, Badoglio faced the prospect of it continuing for another year, as predicted by British and French experts. Thus the news that the Negus had reached the Agumberta Pass to take command of the last Ethiopian army came as a great relief to the Italian Commander-in-Chief, and he immediately cabled to Mussolini: 'Whether the Emperor attacks or whether he waits for my attack his fate is now decided...'

Massacre at Lake Ashangi

In the afternoon of 23rd March 1936 Emperor Haile Selassie gazed across a lush green valley towards the Italian positions at Mai Ceu. Against the advice of his foreign experts and his own better judgement, the Negus had decided not to wait for Badoglio to launch an offensive but to strike first. It was a desperate gesture forced on him by tradition and his chiefs, who saw the only solution of the conflict as a great battle directed by the Emperor in person.

His army of 31,000 men included six battalions of the Imperial Guard and a regiment of artillery equipped with twenty 75mm field guns, some Oerlikon 37's and a few 81mm Brandt mortars. It was undoubtedly the best force that Ethiopia had put into the field. But compared with Badoglio's resources it was pathetically weak. 40,000 Italians and Eritreans were dug in around Mai Ceu. Behind them another 40,000 were distributed between the Belago and Alagi passes. Nevertheless if the Ethiopians had

attacked on 24th March as the Negus had intended, the battle might have gone differently. But in a week that was frittered away in war councils, banquets and prayers, the Italians had worked hard to strengthen their defences and bring up reserves. It also gave them time to bribe the Azebu Galla with thalers and rifles not to fight for Haile Selassie.

The attack was eventually launched at dawn on St George's Day, 31st March. The Italians having been warned by a deserter from the Imperial Guard, had been standing to most of the night and they were ready when the first waves of Ethiopian infantry hurled themselves against the Alpini on the slopes of Amba Bokora, and the Eritreans at the Mekan Pass. The battle began at 0545 hours and it was to continue for thirteen hours with scarcely a break.

Three columns of Ethiopians, each about 3,000 strong, attacked first and in some places the fury of their onslaught carried them into the Italian defences. Accurate and surprisingly devastating mortar fire from the Brandt mortars contributed to these minor successes. But the Alpini fought back, and gradually the situation was stabilised; too late the Ethiopians realised that they should have launched their offensive a week earlier. Unable to break through the line held by the Alpini, they switched their attack to the Mekan Pass and the left flank of the Italian army; there they hoped for less stubborn resistance from the Eritreans. From 4am to 8am Haile Selassie's men kept up a furious onslaught brilliantly supported by the fire of a few machine guns and batteries. At the price of heavy casualties, they achieved a few gains. But at 8am there was an

As the casualty rate soared and major battles continued to be lost, Ethiopia's peasant soldiers began to drift back to their villages. Haile Selassie was forced to launch a great attack, led by himself

ominous roar as Badoglio's bombers flew in from the north. The battle which had been on even terms for more than two hours was over.

At this point Haile Selassie played his trump card, and the Imperial Guard was ordered to attack the Italian left flank. The six battalions of the Negus's elite force were armed with modern weapons and had been trained by European instructors. But they had not yet seen action. Nevertheless their training and discipline was soon apparent in their mode of advance across the open ground. For three hours the Imperial Guard struggled to roll up the Italian flank. In the course of the battle the 10th Eritrean battalion was virtually annihilated. But the Italian battalion commander called down an artillery concentration on his own positions which undoubtedly saved the day.

The battle continued to sway backwards and forwards and some of the Italian forward positions were overrun. But by 4pm it was apparent that the Imperial Guard were not going to capture their objectives. Haile Selassi now knew that his chances of success were poor, but he ordered his troops to attack along the whole front. The sky was heavily overcast and it had started to rain when the three main columns stood up and surged forward again to attack the trenches held by the Alpini. Again they were driven back. The last desperate onslaught lasted about an hour and was directed at the junction of two of the Eritrean battalions. A few trenches fell to the Ethiopians and they did their best to exploit what little success they had. But it was of no use and at 6pm, as the evening began to close in, Haile Selassie ordered his army to fall back. Unfortunately the order came too late; the Ethiopian army was in no condition for an orderly withdrawal. Discipline had broken down in many of the units whose commanders had been killed; the troops had not had anything to eat since before dawn. And as they left the battlefield they were bombed by the Regia Aeronautica, and harrassed by several thousand Azebu Gallas who swooped down like vultures.

That evening, Haile Selassie sent a message to his wife: 'From five in the morning until seven in the evening our troops attacked the enemy's strong positions, fighting without pause. We also took part in the action, and by the grace of God remain unharmed. Our chief and trusted soldiers are dead or wounded. Although our losses are heavy, the enemy too has been injured. The Guard fought mag-nificently and deserves every prais The Amhara troops also did the best. Our troops, even though they ar not adapted for fighting of the Euro pean type, were able to bear com parison throughout the day with th Italian troops.' The Negus had goo reason to be proud of his troops. On captured Ethiopian with a bulle wound in the head who was interro gated by the Italians obviously ha not long to live. But he faced hi captors with dignity. 'Who are you he was asked. 'The commander of thousand men.' 'Why don't you li

lown on that stretcher? The Italians do not harm their prisoners.' 'I prefer to die on my feet. We swore to the Negus that we would capture your positions, or die in the attempt. We have not won, but we have died. Look. . !' And the Ethiopian pointed to the valley littered with corpses.

Ethiopian casualties in this battle of Mai Ceu have been put at something between 1,000 and 8,000 killed. Italian losses were sixty-eight officers and 332 Italian rank and file killed and wounded; 873 Eritreans were also recorded as casualties. The figures speak for themselves. Although the Alpini fought gallantly and the unusually high number of officer casualties is a tribute to their leadership, what Badoglio called 'the battle for the empire' was won by the black colonial troops. As Mussolini had hoped that Italian casualties in Ethiopia would demonstrate that the national character had been rein-

Italian askari machine gunners resist Haile Selassie's Imperial Guard (Ethiopia's crack formation) at the battle of Mai Ceu

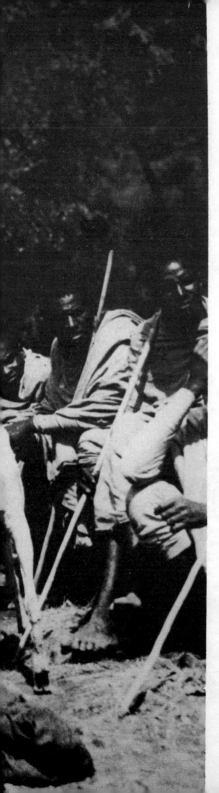

vigorated by Fascism, the fact that so few Italians had fallen was a source of grief.

There was not much sleep for either Haile Selassie's men or Badoglio's troops that night. On the one side of the valley only three of the Red Cross hospitals had moved up to Mai Ceu with the Ethiopian army, and they had either been bombed out of existence or had lost their staff during the battle. In consequence the plight of the Ethiopian wounded was pitiful. Throughout the hours of darkness efforts were made to rescue some of these wretched individuals, and many of the dead were burned under the supervision of the Coptic priests. Meanwhile on the other side of the valley, the Italians worked feverishly to repair their defences in readiness for an attack on the following morning. But the attack failed to materialize and dawn on 1st April 1936 found the Ethiopian army preparing to set out on what was to be an endless retreat.

When the Ethiopian warriors picked up their weapons to march south towards Lake Ashangi and Quoram, few of them had tasted food for more than thirty-six hours. Italian bombers had prevented any supplies getting through to them by bombing anything which moved and by spraying the roads and tracks leading to Mai Ceu. When a thin screen from the better organised Ethiopian units had been deployed to cover the retreat, the Negus gave the order to move. He had not given up all thought of resistance, but by this time he had decided that the only course open to him was to resort to guerilla tactics.

Before the sun had risen on 3rd April some 20,000 survivors of Haile Selassie's once proud army were straggling towards Lake Ashangi carrying the wounded on crude litters. The men were so exhausted and their

Radio-communications, another instance of Italy's overwhelming technological superiority

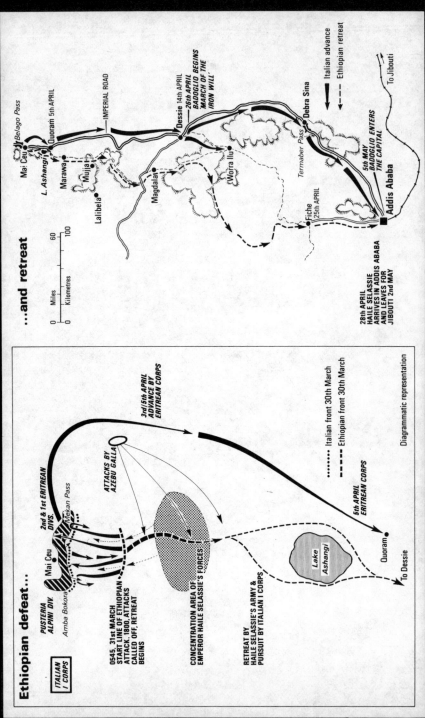

Ethiopian defeat...

ITALIAN
I CORPS

PUSTERIA ALPINI DIV.

2nd & 1st ERITREAN DIVS.

Mai Ceu

Amba Bokora

Mekan Pass

3rd/5th APRIL
ADVANCE BY
ERITREAN CORPS

ATTACKS BY
AZEBU GALLA

0545, 31st MARCH
START LINE OF ETHIOPIAN
ATTACK. 1800, ATTACKS
CALLED OFF, RETREAT
BEGINS

CONCENTRATION AREA OF
EMPEROR HAILE SELASSIE'S FORCES

RETREAT BY
HAILE SELASSIE'S ARMY &
PURSUIT BY ITALIAN I CORPS

Lake
Ashangi

To Dessie

5th APRIL
ERITREAN CORPS

Quoram

Italian front 30th March

Ethiopian front 30th March

ERITREAN CORPS

Diagrammatic representation

...and retreat

Italian advance

Ethiopian retreat

Belago Pass

Mai Ceu

Quoram 5th APRIL

L. Ashangi

IMPERIAL ROAD

Marawa

Mujja

Lalibela

Magdala

Dessie 14th APRIL

26th APRIL
BADOGLIO BEGINS
MARCH OF THE
IRON WILL

Worra Ilu

Termaber Pass

Debra Sina

Fiche
25th APRIL

5th MAY
BADOGLIO ENTERS
THE CAPITAL

Addis Ababa

To Jibouti

Miles
Kilometres
0   60
0   100

28th APRIL
HAILE SELASSIE
ARRIVES IN ADDIS ABABA
AND LEAVES FOR
JIBOUTI 2nd MAY

morale so low that they no longer responded to orders but stumbled along the difficult mountain tracks like automata. The chiefs had already begun to give vent to accusations and recriminations. 'These Imperial Guards', one of Ras Kassa's sons declared bitterly, 'are no better than our simple soldiers – and how much money has been spent on them!' Because the sky was overcast, poor visibility kept the Italian bombers on the ground. But another and more insidious enemy was waiting to pounce: the Azebu Galla. From the rocky heights they fired on the stragglers, and then swarmed down to despoil and mutilate the dead and the wounded. The Azebu Galla served the Italians well during the retreat from Mai Ceu and Badoglio lavished praise on them afterwards.

The sky was cloudless on the morning of 4th April; worse still the approaches to Lake Ashangi were devoid of cover. Nevertheless the Ethiopians resumed their march at first light, and the long column of men debouched from the comparative safety of the Agumberta Pass and moved across the open plain towards the lake. The Ethiopians were afraid they might be cut off and were anxious to put as many miles as possible between the Italians and themselves. (According to Marcel Griaule, the French writer of *Une victoire de la civilisation*, leaflets dropped from an Italian plane, the night before, also contributed to the Ethiopians' lack of caution. 'You can proceed south', the leaflet is reputed to have said. 'Our quarrel is . . . not with you. Rest at night and march during the day. There is no need to conceal yourselves – we shall not attack you.') When the column came in sight of the lake it divided, with the advance guard heading for the eastern shore and the main body taking a route that would bring it to the western side. It was a glorious morning, and doubtless the survivors of Mai Ceu were dreaming of the quiet and peaceful eucalyptus groves of Quoram that lay ahead, when the first wave of bombers roared in to unleash a tornado of destruction.

Squadron after squadron of bombers flew in to hammer the Ethiopian column heading for the eastern shore of the lake, towards which the Eritrean Corps was advancing. Seventy-three tons of high explosives were dropped on the hapless Ethiopians before other aircraft flew in to spray the area with mustard gas. Men and animals were blown to bits or fatally burned. The deadly rain of gas completed the carnage that the bombs had begun. Throughout the day the planes continued to bomb the routed and demoralized force that no longer had any fire in its belly. Describing the scene, Haile Selassie said 'It was no longer a war for the Italian airmen – it was a game . . . It was a massacre . . .' (*Une victoire de la civilisation,* pp 45). Indeed it was a massacre. When evening closed in and the last of the planes flew back to the Italian base at Makale, the plain of Lake Ashangi was strewn with thousands of corpses.

The Negus, who had sheltered in a cave during the attacks, was torn by conflicting emotions of horror, anguish, despair and anger when he looked out at dawn on 4th April and saw the shores of the lake ringed with bodies. During the night the wounded, panting with thirst, had crawled down to drink the gas-contaminated water, and many of them had succumbed to its poison. But there was no time for emotionalism. Soon after the survivors had regrouped and resumed the march towards Quoram a messenger brought news that the Eritrean Corps had got there already. So the column turned right to make for Dessie via the caravan routes and not by the easier Imperial road. As Haile Selassie's men avoided this main road and only marched at night it was several days before they were spotted by Italian reconnaissance planes. But the Azebu Galla were quick to pick up the trail and the rear guard was harried continuously as far south as Marawa. The Negus, who recovered his poise within twenty four hours, believed that it might be possible to make a stand at Dessie where ammunition and supplies had been accumulated in anticipation of protracted operations on the northern front, and where the heir to the throne, Prince Asfa Wossen had been sent to raise a new army.

When the column reached Mujja, however, Haile Selassie suddenly decided to make a pilgrimage to the holy city of Lalibela. This was a useless and dangerous diversion, which was to take several days. Yet the impulse reflects the strange and complex character of the Ethiopian Emperor, and despite the protests of his chiefs the Negus persisted in his mission, and at dusk on 12th April he reached the city, famous for its rock churches. When he entered the largest of these the Coptic priests hastened to pay homage. But he knelt and began to pray. For two days the head of an empire which was about to topple sought to renew his spiritual strength, and during this time not a morsel of food nor a drop of water passed his lips.

The pilgrimage ended on 15th April when the Negus left Lalibela and rejoined what was left of his army plodding on towards Dessie. Near Magdala the scene of a former emperor's defeat at the hands of the British, it was learned that Prince Asfa had abandoned the city on 14th April without firing a shot, and that it had been occupied by the Eritreans. So the column headed for Worra Ilu, but fifteen miles from there runners brought the news that Worra Ilu had also fallen to the Italians. The next objective was Fiche which was reached by a forced march along devious

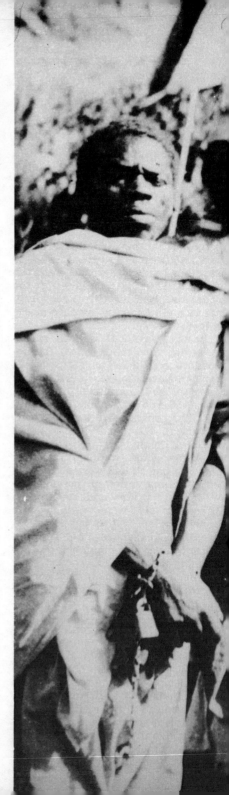

Ethiopian prisoners, chained together and guarded by askaris. The defeat of Haile Selassie's force degenerated into a rout, which in turn became a massacre

Members of the Azebu Galla tribe, bribed with thalers and rifles to harass the retreating Ethiopians

routes on 28th April. A motorable road terminated at Fiche, and vehicles were commandeered to take Haile Selassie and a few of his court dignitaries to Addis Ababa. And so, after an absence of four months the Negus returned to his capital. Addis Ababa was already a city of panic when he arrived on 29th April, with the station besieged by Ethiopian officials an‹ foreigners anxious to get away t‹ Jibuti before the Italians arrived.

Meantime Badoglio had trans ferred his headquarters to Dessie having been flown there on 20th April According to his memoirs the popula tion of this city that had been Hail‹ Selassie's headquarters for many months greeted him 'in a manner tha‹ was truly solemn and festive'. Th‹ Italian Commander-in-Chief was nov only about 200 miles away from Addi‹

the most powerful mechanized column ever to appear on an African road. On the morning of 26th April, three days before the Emperor's return to his capital, 12,500 Italian troops climbed into the trucks and left Dessie for what Badoglio termed the 'March of the Iron Will'. Besides the trucks filled with men, there were vehicles carrying 193 horses; at the gates of Addis Ababa, the Marshal and his staff were to leave their cars and ride in triumph into the capital on horseback.

To protect the mechanized force, Badoglio had sent two 4,000-strong columns of Eritreans forward by route march on 24th April. But the only enemies they encountered were rain and mud, and so the precautionary measure proved to be superfluous. Even at the Termaber Pass, where Badoglio had expected some show of resistance, all was quiet, though the mechanized column had to halt here for two days – but this was due to a section of the road having been demolished. In effect 'The March of the Iron Will' turned out to be little more than a logistic exercise on a grand scale. It was, in the words of an anonymous journalist, 'far more of a sports event than a page in military history'.

Once through Selva Sina, the Italians found themselves in one of the most beautiful and fertile regions of Ethiopia. In the open trucks the men with their rifles between their knees gazed over it spellbound. 'At last', they told themselves, 'we have a worthwhile colony of our own. Most of them were simple peasants and now that the war was over they looked forward to laying down their rifles to pick up spades and reap their reward from the rich black earth that had only known archaic wooden plows. By the time they reached the gates of Addis Ababa, the Italians were almost delirious with joy. Not one of them foresaw that their war was to continue for another five years and that their 'day of the spade' would never dawn.

baba and there was no army left to oppose him. Except for a pitiful procession of refugees, his road was clear. In consequence he decided to risk an advance on the capital with a mechanized column; thanks to General Dall'Ora's genius for organization, this was assembled in Dessie between 21st and 25th April. With 1,785 cars and trucks, Fiats, Lancias, Alfa-Romeos, Fords, Chevrolets, Bedfords and Studebakers, a squadron of light tanks and eleven batteries of artillery this was

The battle of Ogaden

On the southern front the ambitiou Graziani had watched Badoglio's suc cessful progress with jealousy and resentment. Believing that his superio officer had no intention of sharing th laurels of victory with him, Graziani was anxious to establish his own ability. To do this he was determine to launch an offensive against Ra Nasibu's army, deployed in defence o Daggahbur, Jijiga and Harar. As fa back as 25th January he had appeale to Mussolini for reinforcements an supplies. But the vehicles he neede were slow to arrive, and it was the en of February before the Libyan divisio he had asked for to replace th Eritrean division, depleted by de sertions, reached Somaliland. Apar from delays Graziani also faced th problem of setting up an operationa base hundreds of miles from the coast New roads had to be built, and all th essentials needed by an army in th field which would have to advanc more than 200 miles through virtua desert had to be stock-piled.

While Graziani was wrestling with these logistical difficulties Mussolini grew impatient. How long would it be before Graziani started to move forward, he wanted to know. And Badoglio sent a telegram reminding his subordinate that 'audacity pays handsome dividends'. Graziani, seething with rage at what he considered a malicious swipe, replied congratulating Badoglio on his victories in the Tigre, and adding tartly that he could have annihilated the Ethiopian forces in the Ogaden and brought the war to an end long ago, if his superiors had supported him when he first suggested an offensive twelve months before. Badoglio did not reply immediately, and when he did the jibe was ignored. 'Please inform me when you propose to attack Ras Nasibu', he signalled. 'If Your Excellency has already launched the offensive, please let me know the location of your headquarters, so that I can maintain telegraphic contact with you.' Furious, Graziani wired back, 'I do not intend to leave anything to chance in an operation which calls for meticulous preparations . . .' Then, in order to conciliate Mussolini, – who, as usual, expected plans that had been barely drafted to materialize immediately – Graziani sent a cable to Rome, telling the Duce that his offensive would be directed against Harar and that it would be preceded by a series of aerial bombardments. The bombing started on 22nd March, and between that date and the end of the month the Regia Aeronautica on the southern front reduced Jijiga to ruins, and – although it had been declared an 'open' city – much of Harar too.

But this was not enough to satisfy Mussolini, and on 1st April Graziani received another message couched in true *squadristi* terms and impressing on him the need for action. 'Instinct tells me', the Duce cabled, 'that the time is ripe to give Nasibu the flogging he deserves.' Next day Badoglio, who was quietly enjoying his success at Mai Ceu, also attempted to spur Graziani on. 'Imperial army retreating south', he wired, 'I Army Corps and Eritrean Corps, as well as the air force, sent in pursuit. Time has now come to stake all on a final throw. Am sure your Excellency will profit to the full from this situation.' These two cables led Graziani to announce that he would launch his attack on 18th April. Mussolini, seething with impatience, urged him to attack several days earlier, while Badoglio exhorted him sarcastically: 'Graziani, my old comrade-in-arms, make a vigorous beginning that will bring us yet another victory.'

Graziani's troubles were only just beginning. During the first week of April the start of the rainy season transformed streams into raging, swirling torrents and tracks into morasses of squelching mud. General Nasi, who had had many years of service in Africa, advised Graziani not to attempt an offensive in such adverse conditions. But Graziani could not afford to wait, especially as there were reports that the Ethiopians had decided to forestall his offensive and attack the Italians while they floundered in the mud. (In fact a force of 10,000 men under Ras Desta's brother had moved up to the Gorrah Wadi on 8th April, and were digging in on the left bank.)

Although his troops were not ready to move and the swollen rivers were almost impassable Graziani launched his offensive on 14th April. Facing him was Haile Selassie's last army, which – thanks to the existence of a motorable road between Berbera and Jijiga – was better equipped and better supplied than those that had been defeated. Apart from the garrisons of Jijiga and Harar, and the force at the Gorrah Wadi, most of Ras Nasibu's

An Ethiopian corpse marks the beginning of the last major battle of the war when, on 14th April, Graziani attacked Ras Nasibu's army which was established behind the 'Hindenburg Wall'

force of 28,000 men was established behind what was termed the Hindenburg Wall. This so-called 'Wall' was a series of entrenched positions and it was a formidable obstacle. Wehib Pasha, its architect, had made brilliant use of the ground and exploited to the full every military engineering technique of the day. Machine guns had been located to produce a deadly crossfire, the trenches had been connected with crawl trenches and provided with overhead cover, while thick barbed wire entanglements presented a impressive barrier to an approaching enemy.

To smash this line Graziani employed an army of 38,000 men, of whom 15,600 were Italians. In comparison with the massive force Badoglio had deployed at the battles of Tembien and Enderta, Graziani's army was on the small side, but it had the advantage of being almost completely mechanized and had the support of an air force empowered to inflict the maximum losses on the enemy, and above all, shatter his morale. On 14th April Graziani launched a three-pronged attack on Ras Nasibu. The first column, commanded by General Nasi, was to break through the Ethiopian defences at Janogoto, and move rapidly to Dagahamodo and threaten the Ethiopian left flank; the central column, commanded by General Frusci, was to move forward via Hamanlei and Sassabaneh to Daggahbur, the pivotal point of the Hindenburg Wall; while the third column, commanded by General Agostini, was to proceed to Kurali and engage the Ethiopian right flank.

On the very day that his three attacking columns had begun their advance along a 120 mile front Graziani received a telegram from Mussolini

The caves which honeycombed the Gorrah Wadi caused the Italians great difficulty. To eliminate them General Nasi was compelled to bring up tanks and flamethrowers to within a few yards of their entrances

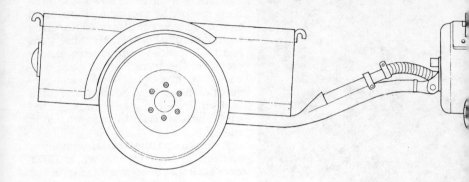

The Italian CV 3/35 was the result of the purchase from Britain in 1929 of a number of Carden Loyd Mark IV tankettes. The basic design was adapted for Italian requirements by a combined team from Fiat and Ansaldo, and first appeared in 1933 as the CV 3/33. The CV 3/33 and CV 3/35 generally similar except for the provision of two machine guns in the latter (with the option of a flamethrower instead of the second gun) or a bridging device instead of the single gun of the CV 3/33. The CV 3/35 later became the L/35 or L3-35. Both versions proved very successful in Ethiopia, where their cross-country ability and limited firepower was more than a match for anything that the Ethiopians could bring against them. The CV 3/35 was armed with two machine guns, weighed 3.85 tons, had a crew of two, armour ranging from 5mm to 14mm in thickness and a top speed of 26mph on the 43hp produced by its SPA 4-cylinder engine

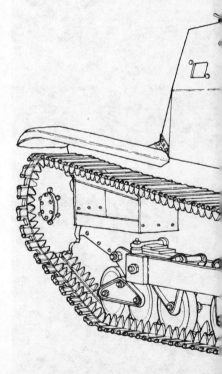

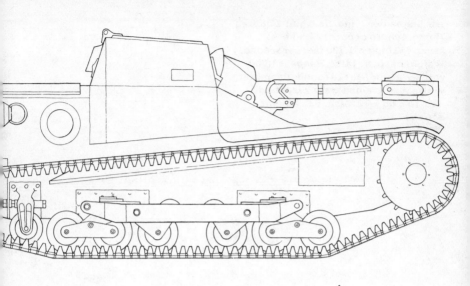

The CV 3/33

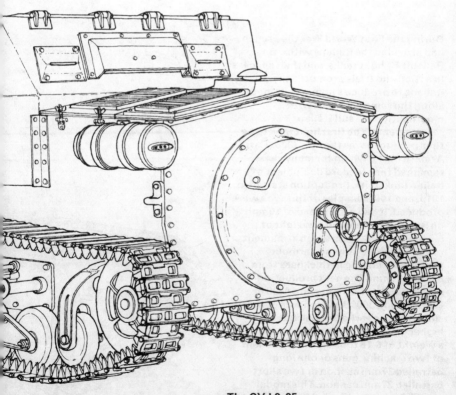

The CV L3-35

The Schneider 75mm field gun. *Calibre :* 75mm. *Length of bore :* 27 calibres. *Muzzle velocity :* 1,730 feet per second. *Weight of shell :* 14lbs. *Range :* 11,000 yards. *Rate of fire :* 20 rounds per minute with a well-trained crew. *Elevation :* −15° to + 65°. *Traverse :* 52°. *Weight in action :* 1 ton

During the First World War the French had provided the Italians with a few Renault FT light tanks, and their success in action and trials prompted the Italians to produce a home-built model along the same lines, but with modifications to suit Italian requirements. The first light tank to be thus produced was the Fiat 3000 (Carro Armato M21), which for many years remained the standard equipment of Italian tank units. Production started in 1919, and 100 examples of this type were produced. It had a top speed of 10mph on its 54hp Fiat engine, a weight of 5.5 tons, a crew of three, an armament of two machine guns and armour protection varying in thickness from 6mm to 16mm. The next production model was the Carro Armato M30 or Fiat Ansaldo 3000B, which was generally similar to the earlier model, but had a higher-powered engine, a crew of two, a weight of 6.18 tons and an armament of two machine guns or one long-barrelled 37mm cannon or two short-barrelled 37mm cannon. This model went into production in 1928

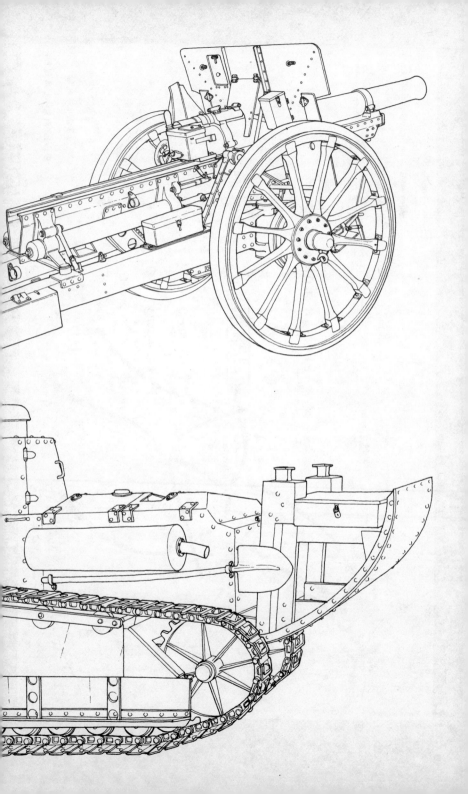

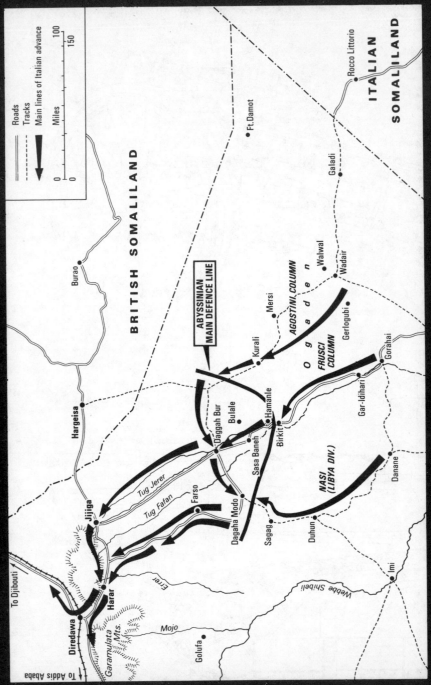

Graziani's advance through the Ogaden

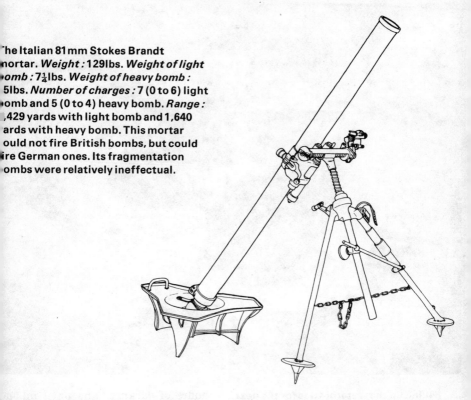

The Italian 81mm Stokes Brandt mortar. *Weight :* 129lbs. *Weight of light bomb :* 7¼lbs. *Weight of heavy bomb :* 15lbs. *Number of charges :* 7 (0 to 6) light bomb and 5 (0 to 4) heavy bomb. *Range :* ,429 yards with light bomb and 1,640 ards with heavy bomb. This mortar ould not fire British bombs, but could ire German ones. Its fragmentation ombs were relatively ineffectual.

hat caused his cup of bitterness to verflow. 'Today, April 14th' the signal ead, 'our advance guards will reach essie. Even on the international ene the rhythm of events is acceler- ting. There is not a moment to lose y dear Graziani. I await the news at you have begun your offensive n Harar.' In his reply Graziani made o attempt to hide his resentment. He eproached the Duce for not taking ccount of the enormous difficulties cing the Italians on the southern ont, and concluded by giving full nt to his feelings: '. . . you have ounded me by insinuating that I am eaf to your explicit demands for tion and the tacit demand of the ntire country which, fully aware of y character, is undoubtedly asking hy I have not swept forward with my stomary energy and vigour . . .'
The first day of the advance passed neventfully. At dawn on 15th April

however, as the Nasi column came within sight of Janogoto, it was brought to a halt by intense fire from the right bank of the Gorrah Wadi. The rain was pelting down and the swirling torrent reinforced the al- ready solid Ethiopian line of defence. The advance guard was composed of Libyan troops, who were wary and thoroughly versed in the insidious ways of desert warfare. Taking stock of the situation they resorted to their patient Bedouin tactics of firing only a few shots and assessing the terrain held by the enemy while making full use of their own. Not a yard of ground was gained during the hours of day- light; while from the caves that honeycombed the rocky peaks of the Wadi, the Ethiopians continued to blaze away. But when dusk fell and the flood water began to ebb a few platoons of Libyans managed to ford the torrent and establish a bridge-

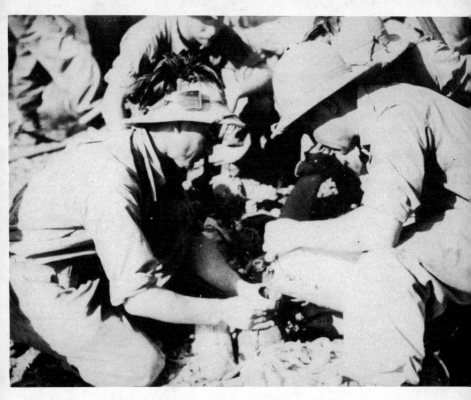

Filling up the waterbottles for the next stage of the Italian advance

head. Nevertheless by dawn on 17th April only part of the Libyan division had succeeded in crossing the Gorrah owing to the 'stubborn resistance' of the Ethiopians. To break it down, General Nasi was compelled to bring up tanks, flamethrowers, and artillery to within a few yards of the entrances to the caves.

After three days of desperate fighting the Ethiopians were forced to withdraw, leaving a couple of thousand dead behind them. Few prisoners were taken. The Libyans were Muslims and they vented their religious hate on the Christian warriors who fell into their hands.

The Nasi column reached the wells of Birkut on the evening of 18th April. But shortly after midnight the Ethiopians launched a surprise attack. Bitter fighting continued through the

hours of darkness and until midda on the 19th. But in the daylight, whe the Italians were able to call on th support of their artillery and aircraft Ras Nasibu's men stood little chance Meanwhile Generals Frusci and Agc stini, whose columns were advancin through torrential rain in the centr and on the right respectively, ha met no opposition and had succeede in reaching their objectives. On th evening of 23rd April all three column had taken up their positions befor the Hindenburg Wall. Nasi's advanc guard, thanks to the fact that it wa mechanized, had outdistanced th main column and reached Dagaha modo; the Frusci column was withi sight of the fortifications of Hamanle and the Agostini column had mad contact at Gunu Gadu. At the firs light of dawn on 24th April, as Marsha Badoglio began his 'March of the Iro Will' fierce fighting broke out on th entire length of the Ogaden fron

From his headquarters in Bulale, Wehib Pasha directed the course of the battle. Nasibu's Turkish adviser had taken into account the 'traditional tactics of war' of the Ethiopians and had trained them in the method of 'offensive' defence. Thus, at dawn on the 24th, it was the Ethiopians who – in the hope of relieving the pressure on their fortified line of defence – attacked along the whole of their front.

Against the weight of the Italian firepower the Ethiopians could make little progress. But the Frusci column's advance was held up, and Frusci himself was so alarmed about the way the battle was going that at one stage he asked Graziani to divert the Agostini column to ease the pressure on his troops. Graziani refused, and the Libyans lost 600 men in the course of a series of bayonet charges designed to break the fanatical Ethiopian resistance. Meantime the Agostini column had also struck a bad patch. Its advance was held up for a day at the Jerar river by Ethiopians firmly lodged in caves, or in hollows, or dug in among the roots of trees. Not until 25th April were the Italians able to overcome this resistance – and then only at the cost of heavy casualties. The Ethiopians lost some 5,000 men in this ten day battle, but Graziani's own troops also suffered heavily – over 2,000 casualties. Remembering that the usual ratio between Ethiopian and Italian casualties on the northern front was ten to one, this was a very high figure.

After the hard-fought successes of the Frusci and Agostini columns, the Nasi column increased its pressure and inevitably the Hindenburg Wall gave way. The Ethiopians made no

The Italian flag flies over Daggahbur, the pivotal point of the 'Hindenburg Line'. When the line broke Ras Nasibu fled to Jibouti to join Haile Selassie, and his army disintegrated

attempt to stand elsewhere and from then on the only opposition Graziani had to contend with during his march to Jijiga and Harar was the everlasting rain and thick viscous mud. On 3rd May, Ras Nasibu – soon to die of tuberculosis – and Wehib Pasha joined Haile Selassie in Jibuti; abandoned by its Commander and Chief of Staff, the army of the Ogaden disintegrated. Some of its fragments crossed the frontier into British Somaliland, others made for the mountains of Garamulata and Chercha where they were to initiate the first phase of the Ethiopian resistance.

Graziani now had only one aim: to get to Harar before Badoglio reached Addis Ababa. But the rain that had plagued him throughout his campaign had created a sea of mud to block the road to his objective. Had it not been for the rain no doubt he would have ridden into the city on the same day as Badoglio entered the capital, or even a day earlier. As it was, when the southern army did reach Harar there was no triumphal entry. Graziani had stumbled and injured himself while visiting a Coptic church in Jijiga. Perhaps the hatred he showed later towards Coptic clergy stemmed from this incident.

At noon on 9th May Badoglio arrived at Dire Dawa in a train from Addis Ababa. On the station platform Graziani and his entourage were drawn up to meet him. Their ceremonial greeting signified the end of the campaign in Ethiopia and illustrations of what at the time seemed to be a significant historical event appeared on the covers of most of the popular magazines published in Italy. Not all the Ethiopians realised the war was over, but so far as the Italians were concerned their mission was accomplished. The Negus had been vanquished and it was now only a matter of mopping up.

'The March of the Iron Will' – Badoglio's columns close in on Addis Ababa

Italy's victory

During his long trek back from Mai Ceu, Haile Selassie had been pondering on ways and means of continuing the struggle. His main preoccupation was to delay the fall of Addis Ababa as long as possible. Then, he decided, the seat of government would be transferred to Harar, or – if Harar was threatened by Graziani – to Gore. Finally, if the worse came to the worst he would join Ras Imru and organise a guerilla war in the gorges of the Blue Nile and among the rugged mountains of Gojjam.

On 1st May, the Negus called the surviving members of the Imperial Council to his palace in Addis Ababa for a discussion on these plans. These dignitaries listened in grave silence and then retired to consider their Emperor's ideas. Meanwhile Haile Selassie sent for the British Minister, Sir Sidney Barton, and M Bodard, the French ambassador, to tell them that he intended to defend the capital. But it was not to be. The Imperial Council had decided that the best thing the Negus could do now was to go to Geneva and make a last appeal to the free world from the League of Nations' platform. When the Council's conclusion was conveyed to him Haile Selassie flatly refused. But when Ras Kassa and his Empress urged him to

go, and when the officer commanding the capital's garrison told him that his troops were too demoralized to fight, the Negus changed his mind. And when the decision to go to Geneva had been taken it seemed sensible to leave at once.

That afternoon Haile Selassie issued his final orders. The government was to move to Gore and the mayor of Addis Ababa was to remain at his post. The latter was to do what he could to keep order until the arrival of the Italians, and try to ensure that no resistance was offered to them. Having made the essential provisions, it seems the Negus momentarily lost control of himself. According to at least one source he left his palace during the night and gave orders for the sacking of the city after his departure. Whether or not the Negus was temporarily overcome, it is highly unlikely that he would go as far as to sanction looting. Indeed on the morning of 2nd May the police and what remained of the Imperial Guard did their utmost to restrain the mob intent on wrecking and pillaging the city. Only when thousands of demoralised and disbanded soldiers and Galla flocked into the capital were the attempts to maintain law and order abandoned. The xenophobia which had smouldered for so long flared up with overwhelming violence, and the rioters looted and set on fire all the shops owned by Europeans.

Haile Selassie was on his way to

Mussolini decorates an askari sergeant, and then makes a trimphant speech to jubilant crowds in Rome – 'At last Italy has her empire. Will you be worthy of it ?' This was his hour of glory

Jibouti when the first plumes of smoke started to rise from Addis Ababa. In the early hours of the morning of 2nd May he and his Empress had boarded the special train packed with court officials, dignitaries and high-ranking officers, which was to carry him to the French post. Graziani had sent a cable to Mussolini asking for permission to bomb the train, but the Duce refused and the journey to Dire Dawa was uneventful. But the train stopped for several hours while the Negus conferred with his old friend the British consul at Harar, Edwin Chapman-Andrews. To Chapman-Andrews he confided that he was already regretting leaving Addis Ababa and that he hoped to return to Ethiopia to join Ras Desta when his mission had been completed in Geneva. Finally, he boarded the train

again and it chugged away to Jibouti across the Danakil desert. Haile Selassie's five years of exile had begun.

Condemned as a traitor Ras Hailu Tekla Haimanot, the deposed governor of Gojjam, had been an unwilling passenger on the train. But at Dire Dawa he had been released together with other prisoners who the Negus suspected would go over to the Italians when the opportunity presented itself. Needless to say, all of them did do so. A number of chests of gold ingots were also carried out of Addis Ababa aboard the royal train. Eventually these were deposited at Barclay's bank in Jerusalem, and used to maintain the Negus in exile and finance the resistance movement in Ethiopia. News that this gold had been taken out of the country was, of course, grist for the Italian propaganda mill, and most of the Italian newspapers carried stories about the rifling of Ethiopia's treasury.

Back in the capital the Negus's departure was the signal for rioting

4th May 1936. The Italians enter Addis Ababa to scenes of destruction caused by looting and burning mobs

and violence. Wild-eyed mobs stormed through the streets, burning and looting; some even tried to storm the British and French legations where most of Addis Ababa's foreign contingent had taken refuge, but the capital's agony was drawing to an end. Badoglio's mechanized column was approaching, and at 4pm on the afternoon of 5th May the Italians reached the gates. It was raining heavily and every *tukul* on the route was displaying a white flag when the Marshal made his triumphal entry into the city of the King of Kings. A detachment of Ethiopian customs guards presented arms as he drove past, and further on an Italian guard of honour, which had accompanied the advance guard for that purpose, paid him the same compliment. The column drove on to the Kebaba suburb through the deserted and litter strewn streets: there was no question now of stopping to allow Badoglio to use the horses that had been brought up for the occasion.

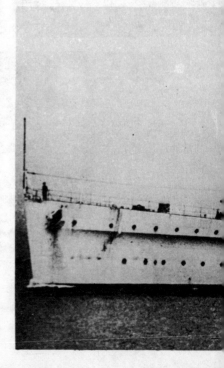

he victors bring civilisation to Addis Ababa – the standard of the Addis Ababa branch of the Young Fascist organisation

Finally the Marshal's entourage pulled up at the Italian legation and at 5.45pm the Italian tricolour was hoisted. Three cheers for King Victor Emmanuel and three cheers for Mussolini followed. Then, turning to the commander of the Regia Aeronautica, Air-Marshal Magliocco, Badoglio said simply, 'We've done it! We've won!'

In Italy, the fall of Addis Ababa had been expected. But when the news that Badoglio had occupied the Ethiopian capital reached Rome late in the evening of 5th May, there were scenes of wild excitement, and jubilant crowds surged into the streets to rejoice. In his speech from the balcony of the Palazzo Venezia the Duce said: 'During the thirty centuries of our history, Italy has known many solemn and memorable moments – this is unquestionably one of the most solemn, the most memorable. People of Italy, people of the world, peace has been restored.' The crowd would not let him go – ten times they recalled him to the balcony and cheered and waved while the boys of the various Fascist youth organizations sang the newly composed 'Hymn of the Empire'. Four days later, the same scenes were repeated when the Duce in a speech about the 'shining sword' and the 'fatal hills of Rome', announced: 'At last Italy has her empire', and asked 'will you be worthy of it?'

This was Mussolini's hour of glory – the moment of his greatest glory, in fact. Intuitively he knew that the Italian nation was united around him as never before, and that the exultation he had just witnessed was genuine, as it had not always been in the

HMS Enterprise leaves Jibouti on 4th May bearing Haile Selassie to the League of Nations

past. And there can be little doubt that the Italian people were united behind the Duce at that moment. While few of them are likely to have paid much attention to the grotesque parallels between the Fascist and Roman empires which he had drawn, they had good cause for rejoicing. The war had been won in far less time than they had anticipated, at a cost of less than 3,000 of their men, and they had acquired a vast territory with untold mineral riches. (Magnified by the regime, of course.) Fascism had never been more popular, and shouts of military glory drowned the muttered grumbles about economic ills.

For Mussolini this was the proudest moment of his life, and the zenith of his climb to success. From then on his course was downward to destruction. Isolated as he was by his defiance of the League of Nations it was inevitable that he would draw closer to the alliance with Hitler that was to prove catastrophic for Italy. The war had bankrupted the exchequer, and the economy was hopelessly unbalanced. But even as the Duce told the world from his balcony that 'Italy wants peace for all' he was preparing for the wanton intervention in Spain which began a few months later. The easy victory in Ethiopia had convinced the Italian generals that Italy had become a great military power overnight; four years later the same generals who had covered themselves with glory in Ethiopia suffered the crushing humiliation of defeat.

While the Italian people were rejoicing Haile Selassie was crossing the Red Sea in the British cruiser *Enterprise*, which sailed from Jibouti during the afternoon of 4th May; his destination was the British mandated territory of Palestine. Two days after his arrival in Jerusalem he sent a telegram to the League of Nations in which he said, inter alia:

'We have decided to bring to an end the most unequal, most unjust, most

The Emperor pleads for his country

barbarous war of our age, and have chosen to take the road to exile in order that our people shall not be exterminated and in order to consecrate ourselves wholly and in peace to the preservation of our empire's independence ... we now demand that the League of Nations should continue its efforts to secure respect for the covenant, and that it should decide not to recognize territorial extensions, or the exercise of an assumed sovereignty, resulting from an illegal recourse to armed force and from numerous other violations of international agreements.'

This telegram dispatched at the right moment caused several governments to defer recognition of the Italian conquest. But it was the Emperor's last success in the diplomatic sphere. Now that the Italians had occupied Addis Ababa, the democracies hoped that the Negus would resign himself to his fate and, as the final act had been played out, allow the curtain to fall. (Britain, in fact, was so anxious to avoid giving offence to Mussolini that, when Haile Selassie reached Gibraltar, he was transferred from the cruiser *Capetown* to an ordinary liner – a ruse by which the British government was spared a state reception.)

Only the hope of gaining the sympathy and support of the world by appearing in person at the rostrum of the League of Nations now remained to the Negus. And so on 30th June 1936 – two months after his defeat at Mai Ceu – Haile Selassie stood before the microphone in the great assembly hall in Geneva. There was a breathless hush as the eyes of all present turned to the slight, diminutive figure in a voluminous black cloak. But the President, M Van Zeeland, had hardly given him the signal to speak when pandemonium broke out in the auditorium. The uproar was caused by twenty or s Italian journalists booing, jeering and yelling insults at the Negus. A Haile Selassie stood there impa sively, waiting for order to be restore Titulescu, the Rumanian chairma jumped to his feet and shouted: 'A l porte les sauvages!' Then, as soon the Italians had been ejected ar silence reigned once more, th Emperor began to plead his cau with infinite courage and pathos: ' Haile Selassie I, Emperor of Ethiopi am here today to claim that justi which is due to my people and th assistance promised to it eight month ago when fifty nations asserted th an aggression had been committe None other than the Emperor ca address the appeal of the Ethiopia people to fifty nations ... Given that

n setting a precedent, that I am the
ˑst head of a state to address the
ssembly, it is surely without prece-
nt that a people, the victim of an
iquitous war, now stands in danger
 being abandoned to the aggres-
ˑ . . .' He then went on to speak of
.e events that had led up to the war
ˑd to denounce the gas attacks made
ˑ the Regia Aeronautica. Ethiopia,
 said, did not expect other nations
 shed their blood for her, but: 'I
ˑsert that the problem submitted to
ˑe Assembly today is a much wider
.e than the removal of sanctions. It
 not merely a settlement of Italian
ˑgression. It is collective. It is the
ˑry existence of the League of
ˑtions . . . in a word, it is inter-
ˑtional morality that is at stake.'
ˑ then turned to the delegates of the
fifty nations, and asked them not to
recognize the Italian conquest but to
grant Ethiopia a loan to finance a
resistance movement: 'Represent-
atives of the world, I have come to
Geneva to discharge in your midst the
most painful of the duties of a head of
state. What reply shall I take back to
my people?'

But the Negus's moving speech
and his prophetic condemnation of
those who were digging a grave for the
ideal of collective security, had no
success, and the Ethiopian resolution
was defeated. Eight days later the
British Home Fleet was recalled from
the Mediterranean, and on 15th July
the sanctions on Italy were lifted.
Mussolini's victory over the Negus
and over the League of Nations seemed
to be complete.

The occupation

Three days after the occupation of Addis Ababa the 50,000 or so Ethiopians who had fled to the mountains of Intoto trickled back to their *tukuls*, and the city began to return to life. The debris and the putrefying corpses were cleared away, and an Italian governor was installed in Haile Selassie's palace. (Six of the Negus' lions which still resided in the palace grounds were promptly shot by the new governor.) Trade started to pick up, the lira was put into circulation, and on the surface all appeared calm. But the war was not over, and the 50,000 strong garrison of Italian and Eritrean troops faced some 50,000 armed but leaderless Ethiopian soldiers. In fact Mussolini's empire was only nominally under Italian domination. About two thirds of the country was still under the control of Ethiopian nobles, and sizeable forces still loyal to Haile Selassie were concentrated in the provinces of Gojjam, Shoa, Jimma, Galla-Sidams and Harage. Some of the chiefs, including Ras Seyoum – whom the Negus had ordered to stir up a revolt in Tigre – surrendered to the Italians, put themselves and their men at Badoglio's disposal and took the oath of loyalty to King Victor Emmanuel. But others like Ras Desta and

Ras Imru were to continue the war in a guerilla campaign.

On 22nd May when Badoglio returned to Italy at his own request, Graziani, the very last man suited to carry out the difficult task of pacifying the country, was appointed Viceroy of Ethiopia. The Duce, knowing him as he did, should have advised Graziani to act with moderation, instead he cabled on 6th June: 'All rebels captured are to be shot.' This gave the new Viceroy all the power he needed and an edict was issued announcing that every Ethiopian who resisted the Italian occupation would be regarded as a brigand. 300 cadets of the Holeta Academy who killed Air – Marshal Magliocco and eleven of his officers when they rashly landed their three planes at Lekemti on 27th June to stir up the pro-Italian Galla against the pro-Haile Selassie Shoans were declared brigands. So were the patriots who repeatedly sabotaged the Addis – Jibouti railway line; so were Ras Desta and his warriors in Galla-Sidamo.

At dawn on 28th July, when Addis Ababa was shrouded by a curtain of torrential rain, a few thousand Ethiopians led by two of Ras Kassa's sons, swooped down from the mountains, surrounded the capital and infiltrated the outlying districts of Kirkos, Bole and Gullale. The Italian troops beat them back almost immediately, but on the following day they attacked again, once more without success. Believing that these attacks had been

Inspired by the Coptic priesthood, the Italians seized the bishop Abuna Petros and summarily executed him in the Addis Ababa market place. Graziani then launched a series of repressive operations, ambiguously described as 'operations of the great colonial policy.' To dispel suspicions about the true nature of these operations Mussolini spoke up in Rome on 24th October. 'It took us seven months to conquer the empire,' he declared. 'But to occupy and pacify it will take us far less time. At this moment our troops are marching hundreds of miles into the fertile regions of the Great Lakes in the heart of Equatorial Africa, while a column of our men is on its way westward to Gore, the seat of the puppet government.' The Duce ignored the fact that almost seven months had elapsed since the occupation of Addis Ababa, and did not mention that during October 1936 173 Italians were killed or wounded; in

Another facet of the pacification programme – an Italian officer teaches at an elementary school in Socota

November the casualty list was 156, in December 134.

If the situation was precarious for the Italian troops, it was desperate for the Ethiopian patriots, who were compelled to live off the land, who had no medical supplies and whose ammunition supplies were running low. Ras Imru with 1,200 men was cut off trying to fight his way back to the Sudan border. Some of his men were wounded, many were sick, and he had only a few rounds of ammunition when he decided to surrender. On this occasion Graziani acted generously; Imru's life was spared but he was deported to Italy to spend seven long years in prison. But when the two sons of Ras Desta responsible for the attacks on Addis Ababa were captured Graziani did not show them the same magnanimity. Both were shot in the town square at Fiche. A few days earlier, Ras Kassa's third son had been captured in the highlands of the Takkaze region and he too had been summarily executed.

The only notables still holding out were Ras Desta and his two chiefs Merid and Maryam – three men who were as slippery as eels, and who managed to elude thousands of Italian and Eritrean soldiers until February 1937. From the end of October 1936 when the trail of Desta's columns was picked up, they and their followers were hounded and harassed around the great lakes of the Jamjamo country, where marshland alternated with dense forests. To avoid being surrounded Desta decided to make for his native province near Addis Ababa but on 19th February he was intercepted by an Italian force. During the ensuing engagement, Maryam was killed, Merid was wounded, taken prisoner and shot with several other chiefs and a number of Eritreans who had gone over to the Ethiopians. Ras Desta himself mana-

Graziani reviews troops. A few days later, on 19th February 1937, there was an attempt to assassinate him. A hand grenade exploded near him and he fell wounded in the back

ged to escape, but five days later the Italians tracked him down to the tiny village of Eya, and he was captured.

The Italians lost no time in arraigning the forty-three year old nobleman before a hastily improvised tribunal, which duly sentenced him to death. The execution by firing squad was carried out immediately after this sentence had been pronounced, and the Italian newspapers printed the news in huge headlines. In the *Gazzetta del Popolo* the editor wrote 'The crack of the firing squad's rifles was a burst of defiant Fascist laughter at the world that so sanctimoniously condemns us, a shot of defiance to the powers who imposed sanctions on us. What a true *squadristi* slap in the face. . . has been administered to that raddled old harlot Geneva.'

But the execution of Ras Desta did not bring the guerilla war to an end,

An Ethiopian hanged after having been accused of participating in the attempt

and as the old leaders were killed off other unknown men took their places. Graziani was driven to such a pitch of fury by the activities of the insurgents that he embarked on a reign of terror. 'We must continue with the work of total destruction', he wired General Pirzio Biroli, 'If a region is not accessible to troops, the air force will clear it, bombing it daily and using all the means at its disposal, essential attack with asphyxiating gases.'

Driven beyond endurance by Graziani's repressive measures, some of the Ethiopians plotted to assassinate him. To celebrate the birth of the Prince of Naples, Graziani had decided to distribute thalers to the neediest inhabitants of the capital. The ceremony took place on 19th February 1937, in the compound of Haile Selassie's old palace and was attended by almost all

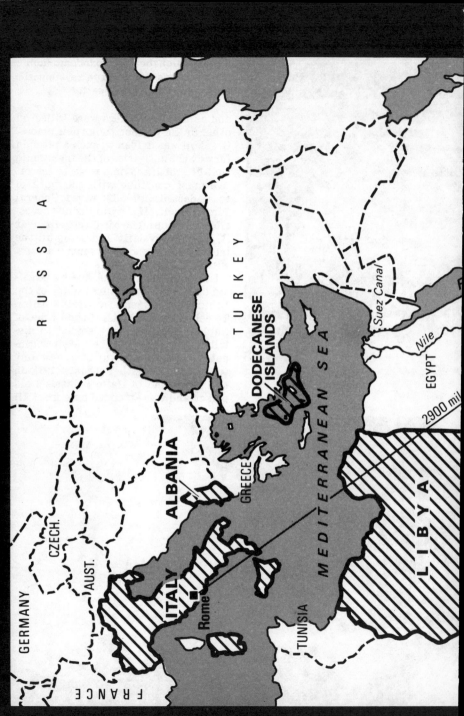

The Italian Empire 1937-1940

Mercator's Projection

Graziani greets the new Viceroy, the humane and cultured Duke of Aosta, before leaving Addis Ababa

the top-ranking Italian authorities in the capital, the Abuna Kyril, and a large numbers of Ethiopian notables. At midday, the poor, of whom there were some 3,000, had just begun to file past the long white table on which the thalers were piled, when a hand grenade hurled by someone hidden in the crowd exploded just above the gate of the palace. A second later, another bomb burst in the midst of the Italian group and Graziani fell, wounded in the back. In the next few minutes, seven more were thrown, injuring General Liotta, Guido Cortese, the mayor of Addis Ababa and another thirty or so people.

The *carabinieri*, convinced that many more missiles would be flung by conspirators lurking in the dense throng, lost their heads and opened fire immediately. The firing went on for three hours and when it stopped the compound was littered with bodies.

But the worst was yet to come. Late that afternoon hundreds of Blackshirts and Libyan askaris gathered outside the palace and then made for the native quarter of Addis Ababa. There they embarked on a systematic

assacre, drenching the *tukuls* with
etrol, setting them alight and
looting the inhabitants as they
merged from the blazing huts. While
his hate ran riot the police kept out
sight, and the massacre went on for
ree days. Then on the morning of
nd February notices were put up
earing the signature of the Italian
ayor Guido Cortese and ordering
eprisals' to cease at noon. The fact
at the authorities issued these
otices was a mute testimony to their
cit acquiescence in the massacre.

Meantime Graziani, unable to trace
is would-be assassins, took advan-
ge of the occasion to liquidate the
tire Ethiopian intelligentsia and all
e prominent young Ethiopians who
d not shown active sympathy
wards the Fascist occupation.
alian newspapers published accounts
the reprisals without any attempt
gloss over the details. In the
azetta del Popolo for 22nd February
37, one report stated that '. . . A
umber of quarters in Addis Ababa
spected for harbouring seditious
ements have been cleaned up by the
quadristi. . .' And two days later, 'Of
e 2,000 Ethiopians taken into cus-
dy after the attempt on the life of
eneral Graziani, several hundred
ere able to prove their innocence and
ave been set free. All those Ethio-
ians found to be armed or in whose
kuls arms were found, have been
xecuted. The rest of the prisoners are
waiting trial.'

How many Ethiopians were killed
this particular blood-bath will
ever be known. The Ethiopians
emselves put the number as high
30,000. English, French, and Ameri-
n newspapers of the day gave
gures which oscillate between 1,400
nd 6,000, while the Italians said that
e total was about 800. But if this
gure is closer to the truth than
e exaggerated number of the Ethio-
ians, it is certain it does not include
e hundreds of Coptic priests and
onks executed on Graziani's orders
the succeeding months. After

the attempt on his life Graziani
regarded all Ethiopians with the
blackest suspicion and his cruelty
undoubtedly led to even more widespread rebellion and finally to his
own removal. Obsessed with hatred
Graziani saw enemies and would-be
assassins wherever he looked and the
story of his Vice-regency is one of
witch-hunts and murder.

In fact there were only two
assassins, Abraham Deboch and Mogas
Asgadom, both of whom were Eritreans and not Ethiopians. Their
'plot' is shrouded in mystery but
many Ethiopians believe that the
motives behind the attempt were
personal reasons associated with the
Fascist 'apartheid' policy which sep-
arated the blacks from the whites.
After hurling their grenades at the
Italian Viceroy they fled and tried to
join one of the Ethiopian guerilla
bands. When the commander of the
freedom fighters would have nothing
to do with them they tried to reach
the Sudanese border but were shot
by unknown Ethiopians before they
could cross to neutral territory.

In Rome the conviction was steadily
growing that even if Graziani had never
uttered his famous phrase, 'The
Duce shall have Ethiopia, with or
without the Ethiopians just as he
pleases', he was putting the second
of these alternatives into practice
with highly undesirable results. Petri-
fied with fear, Graziani rarely emerged from behind the barbed wire
entanglements of the heavily-guarded
Governor's palace, and it was obvious
that a man in his state could not
continue as Viceroy of Ethiopia. Thus
it was to the relief of all, particularly
the Ethiopians, that Graziani was
replaced by a man of a very different
character, the humane and cultured
Duke of Aosta. By way of compensation Graziani was created Duke of
Neghelli, and he left Addis Ababa a
nervous wreck, lamenting bitterly
that he had been unable to trail the
conspirators who had attempted to
assassinate him.

Aftermath and Epilogue

Amadeo, Prince of Savoia-Aosta, Duke of Puglie and Aosta arrived at Massawa in the cruiser *Zara* on 27th December 1937, and two days later was installed as Italy's new Viceroy in Addis Ababa. Before leaving Italy he had been told that Ethiopia had to be pacified, but he was to achieve this end by more conciliatory and humane methods than his predecessor. The Duke, a cultured and liberal-minded man, was by nature ideally equipped for the task of persuading the Ethiopians to accept and co-operate with the Italians but Graziani's behaviour had made the task well nigh impossible.

Even those Ethiopians who had been prepared to accept Italian rule because they realized instinctively that it would lead to the rapid development of their country had been terrorized by Graziani's brutality. Some of these men had taken the oath of loyalty to their new masters now thoroughly distrusted Italian authority; others joined the ranks of the

By the time the Duke of Aosta arrived a new and more insidious war was well under way, a war of skirmishes and ambushes in which Italian military resources and patience were stretched to the utmost

freedom fighters. For the Italians this was a tragic state of affairs. Before the occupation of Addis Ababa there was every reason to believe that Italian propaganda had convinced the majority of Ethiopians that a new era of freedom and prosperity was about to dawn. In consequence they had confidently expected that fruitful collaboration would follow the defeat of Haile Selassie's armies. But Graziani savage and indiscriminate reprisa and the liquidation and deportatio of the Ethiopian intelligentsia ha almost completely disillusioned t remaining Ethiopians, and by t time the Duke of Aosta was install a new form of resistance moveme had sprung up. This came not from t remnants of the Ethiopian armies b

Road building, part of the public works programme which resulted in the construction of 2,000 miles of new roads and twenty-five hospitals

inherited a more disastrous situation. He did all he could to regain the confidence of the Ethiopians, but he had arrived on the scene too late. By September 1937 the resistance movement had assumed alarming proportions, and a new, insidious and more difficult war had begun: a war of skirmishes and ambushes in which the Italian superiority in men and material counted for little. From that time on the Italian press was silent on the subject of military activity in Ethiopia, and the story of Ethiopian resistance from 1938–41 has yet to be written. In these years the insurrection was kept alight by outside support – much of which came from the French who became increasingly conscious of the threat to their tiny colony in Somaliland. During 1937 a good deal of money and arms were smuggled in to the patriot leaders from Jibouti. But when the Italians realized what was happening they kept a strict watch on the frontier and the French had to send their consignments of equipment to Ethiopia via the Sudan. The British were of course aware of these subversive activities but it was not until 1939 that they decided to participate in them. From then on Khartoum became the centre of support for the insurgents.

Haile Selassie, who was living in England, did what he could with the limited means at his disposal to provide for the Ethiopians who had fled from their country. Thousands of them were in the Sudan, and many others had taken refuge in French Somaliland, British Somaliland, and Kenya. When the Second World War broke out these men formed the cadre of the Ethiopian Liberation Army.

om the people themselves who were onvinced that the Italians intended o exterminate them.

Notables and dignitaries who had ianaged to escape from Graziani's utches and members of the Coptic ergy who feared the effects of an alian pro-Moslem policy formed ie nucleus of the movement.

The Duke of Aosta could not have

Outside the towns guerilla activity was rife and in 1937 the Italian military authorities in Ethiopia decided

Blackshirts man a new outpost in the expanding Italian Empire

Alms for the poor. By the beginning of 1939 the tempo of guerrilla war was slackening, and the Duke of Aosta's policy appeared to be winning over the Ethiopians, but the Second World War was soon to radically alter the situation

to build stone forts at intervals along the main roads and to raise native battalions of 500–600 men, commanded by Italian officers – battalions that would use the same tactics as the guerillas. But it was not merely to deal with the insurgents that these native contingents were raised. Mussolini wanted to create a 'black army' powerful enough to defend Ethiopia if it were attacked, and he had envisaged mobilizing some 300,000 Ethiopians by the time Italy's rearmament programme was completed in 1940.

In the main centres of population the Italians kept a tight grip on security. Control was based on a policy which distinguished between the conquering whites and the subject blacks – the colonial policy that ha propagated *apartheid*. But the Italian have never been addicted to racialism they are by nature friendly and charitable, and in Ethiopia they sub mitted with reluctance to the Fascis laws forbidding the two races t intermingle. The architects of th new empire proclaimed a racial hier archy, and severe penalties wer incurred by Italians who infringe these laws; for instance Italians foun guilty of setting-up house with a Ethiopian woman were liable to fiv years imprisonment. But the me who replaced the Shoan overlord went beyond attempts to segregat black from white. They also nurture the hatred of the nomadic Somali for the Ethiopians of the highland and many of the disorders in Eas Africa today have their origins in th

Orde Wingate, later to achieve fame as commander of the Chindits in Burma, whose Gideon Force of Ethiopian patriots . . .

Fascist colonial policy which aimed at establishing a population balance favourable to the Italian programme of demographic colonisation.

Yet there is another side to the coin. Certain that Ethiopia was theirs for good the Italians set about providing Ethiopians with what they lacked: practically everything in fact. And in the space of the five years, which was the life span of their ephemeral empire, they wrought miracles. In five years they endowed the country with two thousand miles of new roads – many of which were asphalted – and twenty-five hospitals, fourteen hotels, dozens of post offices, telephone exchanges, aqueducts, schools and shops were built. Just as in America in the time of the Gold Rush, villages not even on the map became prosperous towns almost overnight. Unfortunately the Second World War brought an end to the existence of many of these towns, and the countless Italian projects were left unfinished. Of these the colonization programme was perhaps the most significant. Mussolini's original intention had been to resettle a million peasants who owned no land in Italy in the fertile regions of the empire as soon as the war finished. In 1937 there was talk of ten million colonists who would transform Ethiopia into the granary of Africa and Europe. But the

constant dangers of the guerilla war
and the clouds gathering ominously
over the political skies of Europe put
a brake on the colonization programme that the Duce had claimed as
one of his main reasons for the war.
Thus, in five years of occupation only
300,000 Italians were absorbed into
Ethiopia and more than a third of
these were soldiers.

The benefits brought to Ethiopia
combined with the Duke of Aosta's
lenient and wise administration did
much to repair the wrongs done by
the Italians. Indeed, by the beginning
of 1939 it was apparent that the tempo
of the guerilla war and the resistance
movement was slackening, and if
Mussolini had not decided to throw
in his hand with Hitler the Italians
might still be ruling Ethiopia.

'Italy has entered the war as the
ally of Germany.' The Italians had
been expecting Mussolini's announcement on 10th June 1940, just as they
had expected the announcement of
the war in Ethiopia. But in 1940 their

reaction was different; it was cold and almost hostile. Even the Duce's customary purple passages, and his rhetorical images of 'blazing British battleships' failed to kindle their enthusiasm. 'The adventure begins – God help Italy', Ciano wrote in his diary.

Three days later a mysterious Mr Strong took off from Poole harbour, on the south coast of England, in a Sunderland flying boat bound for Egypt; Haile Selassie, alias Mr Strong, was on his way home. His journey was as uneventful as it was exciting, and on 25th June the Sunderland touched down at Alexandria. Seven days later the Negus, now transmogrified into Mr Smith, was flown to Khartoum

where, under the direction of General Sir William Platt, a campaign was being planned to free Ethiopia from the Italian yoke.

On 4th July, however, the Italians took advantage of their numerical superiority, and launched an offensive which took them across the Sudan frontier at several points. Encouraged by the minor success on this front perhaps, an Italian army under General Nasi invaded British Somaliland and overran the colony within a few days. But these successes were no more than a show of strength; six months later the Italians were evicted from Somaliland and driven back across the Sudan border. Meanwhile the news of Haile Selassie's return to Africa had reached his people, and given a fillip to the rumbling insurrection whose flames were being fan-

2nd February 1942. Haile Selassie and Sir Philip Mitchell sign the Anglo-Ethiopian Agreement

The Italians retreated to mountain fortresses and dug themselves in

ned by officers of British Mission 101.

The campaign to liberate Ethiopia can only be said to have started when General Platt launched his offensive against Eritrea. But in November, a certain Major Ordę Wingate – who has since been called 'the Napoleon of guerilla warfare' arrived in Khartoum. Under Platt's directions and with Haile Selassie's authority Wingate organized the 2,000 strong Gideon Force of Ethiopian patriots commanded for the most part by British officers. On 18th January 1941, while Platt's troops were preparing to assault Kassala and sweep into Eritrea, Gideon Force reached the little frontier village of Um Iddla. Two days later the Negus joined Wingate, and the standard of the Lion of Judah was raised again in Ethiopia.

In less than three months Gideon Force, swelled by an increasing number of patriots, was advancing towards Debra Markos and the Italians had abandoned Eritrea, Somaliland, and the Ogaden to Platt's troops converging on them from the north, and

an army under General Sir Alan Cunningham advancing from the south. On 6th April Haile Selassie entered Debra Markos and Cunningham occupied Addis Ababa, where some 40,000 Italian civilians feared the sudden return of the Negus might well precipitate a bloodbath. But there were no reprisals and when Haile Selassie rode back into his capital in triumph on 5th May, exactly five years after Badoglio, there was not a single ugly incident to mar the scene. The King of Kings had come home and in his address to the crowds who had gathered to welcome him almost the first words he spoke were: 'My people, Do not repay evil with evil. . . do not stain your souls by avenging yourselves on your enemies...'

Meanwhile the remnants of the defeated Italian armies had retreated to the mountain fortresses of Gondar, Amba Alagi, Dessie and Jimma where they had dug themselves in for a last desperate stand. Amba Alagi, attacked by General Platt's forces on

Harassed all the time by Ethiopian guerrillas, they surrendered in November 1941

The monument celebrating the return of Haile Selassie to Addis Ababa after five years of exile

1st May, was the first to fall, and the Duke of Aosta who was in command of the garrison surrendered within two weeks of Haile Selassie's return to the capital. Three months later the Italians were broken at Jimma and with the surrender of Gondar on 18th November 1941 all Italian resistance in Ethiopia came to an end. The empire, which had been an empire more in name than actual fact, had ceased to exist. In the futile attempt to defend it 5,000 Italians and 10,000 Askaris were killed – almost three times the number killed during the war of conquest.

By the end of June 1936 Italy had spent about twelve billion lire (about £7 million sterling, or $17 million) on the creation of her new empire; her treasury was empty and Mussolini had mortgaged his country's future. Over 2,000 Italians and 1,600 Eritreans had been killed in the campaign. A peace treaty was not signed until 10th February 1947 and diplomatic relations between Italy and Ethiopia were not resumed until 1952.

Following the negotiations for the peace treaty Ethiopia presented Italy with a bill for the damage inflicted on her in the course of the Duce's colonial adventure. The following losses were recorded:

Killed in action	275,000
Patriots killed in battle (i.e. men killed during the occupation 1936-1941)	78,500
Women, children and others killed by bombing	17,800
Massacre of February 1937	30,000
Persons who died in concentration camps	35,000
Patriots executed by sentence of Summary Courts	24,000
Persons who died from privations due to the destruction of their villages	300,000
Total:	760,300

The loss of 2,000 churches, 525,000 houses, and the slaughter and confiscation of 5,000,000 beef cattle, 7,000,000 sheep and goats, 1,000,000 horses and mules, and 700,000 camels was also claimed in this memorandum when the bill for reparations totalling £184,746,023 was presented to the Economic Commission for Italy.

Feeble and ineffective as they had been, when it came to reckoning up the cost of the sanctions applied by the League of Nations, it was clear that they had already affected the economic life of both Italy and the Powers that had applied them. Contemporary estimates put the cost of the war to Europe – excluding Italy – at about £2 million sterling a week (i.e. $600,000 a day). Britain and France calculated that they had lost about 8 million sterling ($20 million) each in trade. Even harder hit by the sanctions policy were the smaller states of south east Europe where trade with Italy represented a much higher proportion of their total than was the case with the Western Powers.

If these material losses had been the only ones suffered by the sanctionist states the balance sheet would not have looked so bad despite their failure to achieve their objective. But the shilly-shallying throughout – especially by France and to a lesser extent by Britain – not only furthered the distrust of their policy that had been growing among the smaller states, but also supplied another object-lesson to the dictators on methods of obtaining what they wanted from the democracies.

And the lesson was not lost on Adolf Hitler, who was just as responsible as anyone else for the spineless handling of Mussolini. It would be an exaggeration to say that the rape of Ethiopia was the direct cause of the Second World War. But there can be little doubt that Mussolini's campaign and the ineffectual response to it favoured the conditions that led to the great conflagration.

Bibliography

Badoglio, Pietro *La Guerra D'Etiopia (The War in Abyssinia)* Methuen & Co, London 1937

Baer, George W *The Coming of the Italian-Ethiopian War* Harvard University Press, Cambridge 1967

Barker, A J *Eritrea 1941* Faber & Faber, London 1966 and *The Civilising Mission* Faber & Faber, London 1968

De Bono, Emilio *Anno XIIII: The Conquest of an Empire* The Cresset Press Ltd, London 1937

Farago Ladislas *Abyssinia on the Eve* G P Putnam, New York 1935

Fuller, Maj-General J F C *The First of the League Wars* Eyre & Spottiswoode, London 1936

Hibbert Christopher *Benito Mussolini. The Rise and Fall of Il Duce* Longmans Green & Company, London 1962

Hollis, M Christopher *Italy in Africa* Hamish Hamilton Ltd, London 1941

Luther, Ernest W *Ethiopia Today* Stanford University Press, Calif. 1958, Oxford University Press, London 1958

Mosley, Leonard *Haile Selassie: The Conquering Lion* Weidenfeld & Nicolson, London 1964

Steer, George L *Caesar in Abyssinia* Little, Brown & Co, Boston 1937, Hodder & Stoughton, London 1936